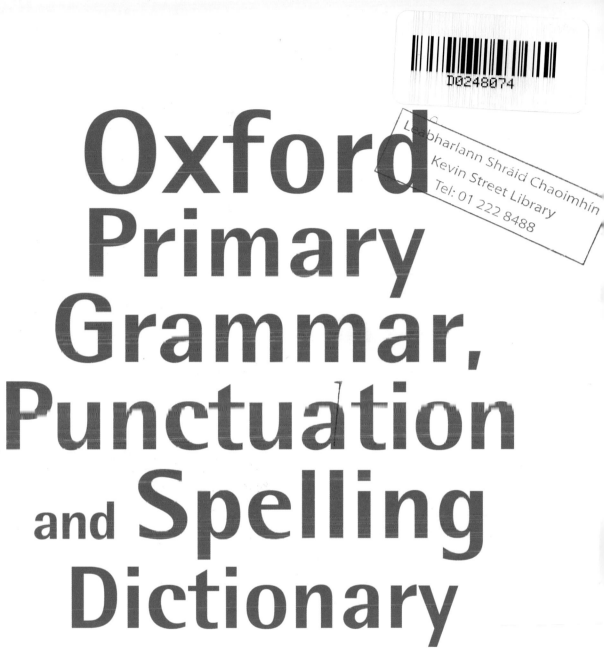

Oxford
Primary
Grammar,
Punctuation
and Spelling
Dictionary

OXFORD
UNIVERSITY PRESS

Great Clarendon Street, Oxford OX2 6DP

Oxford University Press is a department of the University of Oxford.
It furthers the University's objective of excellence in research, scholarship,
and education by publishing worldwide in

Oxford New York

Oxford is a registered trade mark of Oxford University Press
in the UK and in certain other countries

© Oxford University Press 2013

The moral rights of the author have been asserted

Compilers: Fiona Tomlinson and Jenny Watson
Educational consultant: Gill Matthews
Grammarian: Richard Hudson

Database right Oxford University Press (maker)

First published 2013
Updated reprint 2014

British Library Cataloguing in Publication Data

Data available

ISBN: 9780 19 273421 1

10

Printed in Great Britain by Bell & Bain Ltd, Glasgow

Oxford
Primary
Grammar,
Punctuation
and Spelling
Dictionary

OXFORD
UNIVERSITY PRESS

Contents

Introduction

This dictionary will support children aged 7-11 years learning about grammar, punctuation and spelling. The pages are designed to make it easy and fun to use. It is split into two main parts.

The first part deals with grammar, punctuation and spelling rules giving practical tips and examples throughout. All terms and rules are explained in a simple and accessible way. There is also help on how to avoid the most common errors.

EASY TO REMEMBER

★ A **question tag** is a short question on the end of a sentence, used when you want someone to respond to what you have said, e.g. He's a teacher, **isn't he**?

WATCH OUT!

The tense is shown by the verb. It is important to use the correct form.
✗ I **visit** my auntie yesterday.
✔ I **visited** my auntie yesterday.

The second part is an alphabetical spelling dictionary of over 10,000 words that children need to write. It lists words, their word class, and forms spelt out in full. The word selection is backed by the Oxford Children's Corpus, a unique database of children's language which provides important data on the words most frequently used by children. Special attention is given to tricky words including the top 100 misspelt words from the latest analysis from the Oxford Children's Corpus.

All sections are colour coded to make it easy to reference any one area quickly.

There is a comprehensive index of all the key terms at the back of the book.

The publishers would like to thank the primary teachers and schools, the educational consultants and grammarians whose advice and expertise proved invaluable in the compilation of this book.

Grammar

We use words to communicate and we use **grammar** to organize the words. Every word in a sentence has a job to do. If the grammar of a sentence is correct, then the meaning will be clear.

Word classes

Words can do different jobs depending on their **word class**, or part of speech. Adjectives, nouns and verbs are all examples of different word classes.

green bird That my apple took.

These words are all muddled up! It should say: That green bird took my apple.

The words in the sentence need to work together to make the meaning clear.

The word 'green' is an **adjective**.

The word 'bird' is a **noun** and most sentences have a noun or a pronoun.

The word 'took' is a **verb**.

Grammar

A **verb** often (but not always) names an action.

See page 24 for more on tenses.

The bird **pecks** the apple and **eats** it. The bird **is** happy.

action or doing words

being word

If you can make a word into a past tense, it is a verb.

The bird **is** happy because he **likes** apples.

was

liked

More verbs:
| laugh | build | run | hear | enjoy |
| speak | listen | write | play | |

An **adjective** gives more information about a noun. It often goes before the noun or after **is**, **am**, **are**, **was** or **were**.

The **little**, **green** bird pecked the **juicy** apple. The apple was **delicious**.

The adjectives **little** and **green** give more information about the bird and the adjectives **juicy** and **delicious** give more information about the apple.

More adjectives: gorgeous   honest   happy   tiny

A **noun** names a person or thing.

The **bird** pecked the **apple**.

A **common noun** is a noun that refers to people or things in general.

dog   tree   bridge   chair   bread

A **proper noun** is a noun that identifies a particular person, place or thing. Proper nouns begin with capital letters.

James   Africa   Friday

An **uncountable** noun cannot be plural, but a **countable** one can.

Jim spent his **pocket money** on the **tickets**.

uncountable   countable

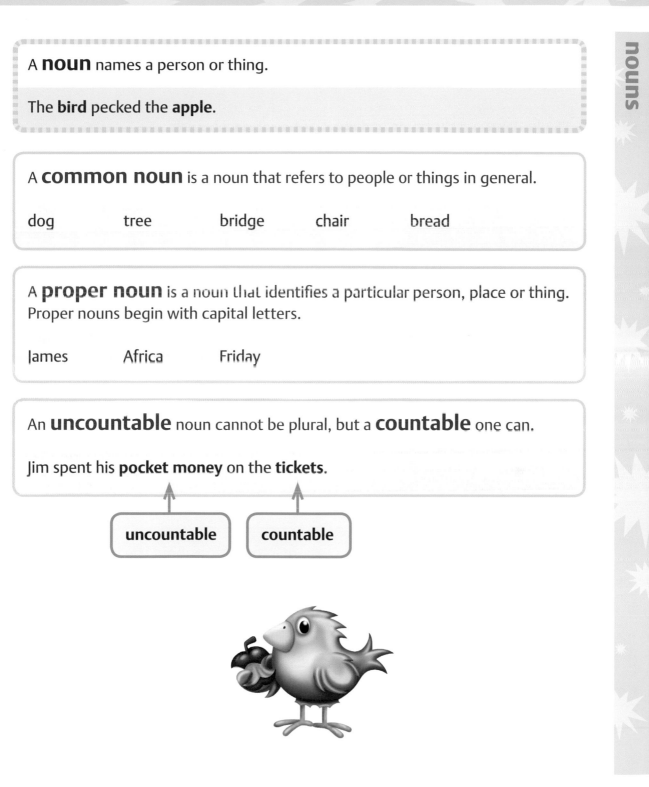

pronouns

A **pronoun** can be used instead of a noun. Using a pronoun avoids repeating the noun again and again.

The bird pecked the apple and ate **it** as **he** sat on a branch.

The pronoun **it** replaces the words 'the apple'.

The pronoun **he** replaces the words 'the bird'.

Possessive pronouns tell you who something belongs to.

This apple is **mine**!

For possessive determiners, see page 14.

The pronoun **mine** shows the apple belongs to the bird.

More possessive pronouns:

mine   yours   his   hers   ours   theirs

Relative pronouns introduce more information about the noun.

The bird **that** sat on the branch was eating an apple.

The relative pronoun **that** introduces more information about the bird.

WATCH OUT!

See page 19 for more on relative clauses.

You can leave out the relative pronoun **that** from some sentences, but not others.

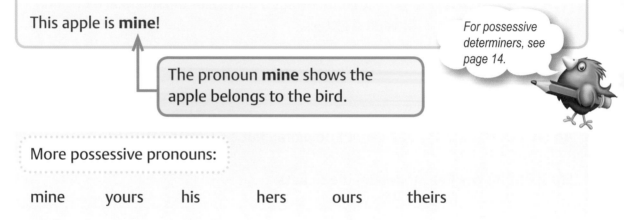

✔ The apple the bird was eating was juicy.
This means the same as: The apple **that** the bird was eating was juicy.

✘ The bird was eating the apple flew away.
This should be: The bird **that** was eating the apple flew away.

More relative pronouns: who   whom   whose   which

Pupils **whose** names are called out must stand up.
The words **where** and **when** are sometimes used as relative pronouns.
This is the house **where** I grew up.

A **conjunction** links words or groups of words within a sentence.

Later, a cat crept up the tree **as** the bird pecked the apple **and** ate it noisily.
The cat watched the bird quietly **because** he didn't want to scare it away.

And joins groups of words which are of the same importance in the sentence – it is called a **co-ordinating conjunction**.

Because joins words or groups of words which are not as important as the rest of the sentence – it is called a **subordinating conjunction**.

Examples of conjunctions:

co-ordinating conjunctions:	and	but	or

subordinating conjunctions:	after	although	as	because
	before	if	since	
	when	while		

An **adverb** gives more information about a verb, an adjective, another adverb or a clause. An adverb tells you how, when, where or how often something happens.

Later, a cat crept up the tree as the little green bird **eagerly** pecked the juicy apple **twice** and ate it **noisily**.

Later gives more information about **when** the cat crept up the tree.

Twice gives more information about the **number** of pecks.

Eagerly and **noisily** give more information about **how** the bird was pecking/eating.

Some adverbs make a comment or link ideas.

Fortunately, we won. **However**, the other team played well.

See page 75 for information about adding **-ly** to adjectives to form adverbs.

Some adverbs are used to say how likely or possible something is.

We'll **definitely** come to the party.
Perhaps he forgot.

WATCH OUT!

See p31 for more on adverbs as cohesive devices.

Some adverbs are used for emphasis.

The bag was **terribly** heavy.   He worked **very** quickly.

A **preposition** usually comes before a noun or pronoun. It often shows place or direction.

Later, a cat crept **up** the tree. Suddenly, the cat tried to pounce **on** the little green bird, but crashed **into** the tree.

Some prepositions show time or cause.

After this, the cat was furious **with** the bird.

More prepositions:

above	against	behind	below	beside	between	in
inside	near	on	off	onto	outside	over
through	under					

WATCH OUT!

It is important to know that words can belong to more than one **word class**.

The word **off** is a preposition and an adverb.
preposition: She fell off the horse.
adverb: She fell off.

The word **this** is a pronoun and a determiner.
pronoun: After this, the cat was furious.
determiner: After this embarrassment, the cat was furious.

The word **bat** is a noun and a verb.
noun: Can I borrow your bat please?
verb: Our team is going to bat first.

A **determiner** goes in front of a noun and its adjectives to help to tell you which person or thing the sentence is about, or how much or how many of them there are.

The little green bird pecked **one** juicy apple and ate it as he sat on **a** branch.

The word **one** tells you how many apples the bird pecked.

The words **the**, **an** and **a** are called **articles** which are a type of determiner. Change **a** to **an** if the next word starts with a vowel.

More determiners:

this	that	these	those
some	any	no	either	neither
each	every		
many	much	few	little	both	all
three	fifty	three thousand	
which	what	whose	

A **possessive determiner** is used in front of a noun to show possession.

my   your   his   her   its   our   their

Auxiliary verbs

Auxiliary, or helping, verbs are used with main verbs. **Be**, **do** and **have** are auxiliary verbs.

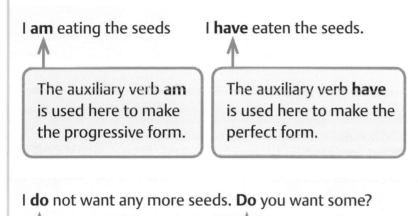

I **am** eating the seeds

The auxiliary verb **am** is used here to make the progressive form.

I **have** eaten the seeds.

The auxiliary verb **have** is used here to make the perfect form.

I **do** not want any more seeds. **Do** you want some?

The auxiliary verb **do** is used in negative statements and in questions.

Modal verbs are a kind of auxiliary verb. They can be used to say what is possible, what is necessary or what is going to happen in the future.

We **might** go to the park today.

I **must** tidy my room or Mum **will** be angry!

will	would	can	could	may
might	shall	should	must	ought to

Sentences

A **sentence** tells you something, asks you something, asks you to do something or exclaims about something.

★ In writing, all sentences start with a capital letter and end with a full stop, question mark or exclamation mark.

★ Sentences consist of one or more clauses.

★ All sentences have a verb and in most sentences, the verb has a subject.

See page 19 for more on clauses, and page 21 for more on subjects.

A statement

I love seeds.

An exclamation

What delicious seeds these are!

A question

Should I eat these seeds?

A command

Take these seeds away!

A sentence that is a command or instruction is usually in the imperative, with the verb first.

Types of sentence

A single-clause sentence consists of one main clause.

The bird ate the apple.

A multi-clause sentence consists of more than one clause.

The bird felt hungry and **it ate the apple**.

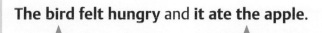

| main clause | main clause |

Although it had already eaten, the bird ate another apple.

subordinate clause

EASY TO REMEMBER

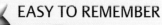

A main clause is a clause that can be used on its own as a sentence.

A subordinate clause often starts with a conjunction such as **although**, **because** or **when**.

A subordinate clause cannot exist on its own.

✗ Although it had already eaten.
✔ Although it has already eaten, the bird ate another apple.

Phrases

A **phrase** is a group of words that can be understood as a unit. A phrase is not a sentence.

A **noun phrase** has a noun as its head, or key word.

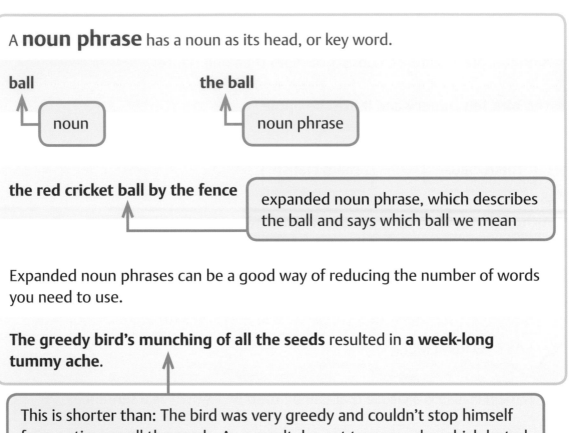

ball

noun

the ball

noun phrase

the red cricket ball by the fence

expanded noun phrase, which describes the ball and says which ball we mean

Expanded noun phrases can be a good way of reducing the number of words you need to use.

The greedy bird's munching of all the seeds resulted in **a week-long tummy ache**.

This is shorter than: The bird was very greedy and couldn't stop himself from eating up all the seeds. As a result, he got tummy ache which lasted for a whole week.

A **preposition phrase** is a preposition followed by a noun or noun phrase.

See pages 8-13 for more on nouns, adjectives, prepositions and adverbs.

I waited quietly **behind the tree**, ready to jump out.

Clauses

A **clause** is a phrase which has a verb as its head, or key word. The other words add meaning to the verb.

If a clause works on its own as a sentence, we say that it is a **main clause**.

The bird pecked the apple. It flew away.

verb   verb

Main clauses can be joined with co-ordinating conjunctions such as **and**, **but** and **or**.

The bird pecked the apple and **It flew away.**

A **subordinate clause** helps to give more meaning to the main clause. It cannot exist on its own as it is not a complete sentence. A subordinate clause often starts with a subordinating conjunction such as **although**, **because**, **before**, **if**, **since** or **when**.

The bird pecked the apple **before it flew away**.

This is the subordinate clause. It is not a sentence on its own but tells you when the bird pecked the apple.

A **relative clause** is a type of subordinate clause. It is connected to the main clause by a relative pronoun such as **that**, **which**, **who**, **whom** or **whose**.

See page 10 for more on pronouns.

I enjoyed the film **that we saw last night**.

Adverbials

An **adverbial** is a word or phrase which gives more information about a verb or about a clause. An adverbial can be an adverb, a phrase or a subordinate clause.

Adverbials tell you about time, place, manner or number and answer these questions:

Where?	When?	How?	Why?
How often?	How long?	How much?	

The dog slept **under the table**.
Jack worked **very hard**.
The cat sleeps **all day**.
I **usually** do my homework before I watch TV.

Adverbials often appear at the end of the sentence, but sometimes they appear at the beginning. These are called **fronted adverbials**. There is usually a comma after a fronted adverbial.

First thing in the morning, I walk the dog.
Next, I have my breakfast.

Some adverbials link ideas across paragraphs or within paragraphs. These adverbials are often fronted.

See page 32 for examples of adverbials linking ideas.

on the other hand   in contrast   as a result   secondly

adverbials • fronted adverbials

Subject, verb and object

All sentences have a **verb**.

The bird **pecked** the apple.

verb

The apple **was** juicy.

verb

The **subject** of a verb is often who or what does or is something (the do-er or be-er). In a statement, the subject is usually the noun, noun phrase or pronoun just before the verb.

The bird pecked the apple. **It** was juicy.

subject

subject

Sometimes a verb has an **object** as well as a subject. The object is who or what is acted upon by the verb. In a statement, the object is usually the noun (or noun phrase or pronoun) just after the verb.

The bird pecked **the apple**.

object

In some sentences the verb is followed by a description of the subject. This is called the **complement**. The verb **be** usually has a complement.

The bird was **hungry**.

In this sentence, **hungry** is the complement. It describes how the subject feels.

Sometimes there can be more than one person or thing doing the action in a sentence.

Zac and **I** are cycling to school.

You use **I**, not me, when you talk about **yourself** as the person doing the action.

Susan and **me** played with Kate. ✘
Susan and **I** played with Kate. ✔

Harry and **me** love pizza! ✘
Harry and **I** love pizza! ✔

EASY TO REMEMBER

Check if you should use **I** or **me** with this simple trick! Your sentence should still make sense if you take out the other person's name and the word 'and'.

Sally and me walked to Selma's house. ✘
Sally and **I** walked to Selma's house. ✔

Me walked to Selma's house. ✘
I walked to Selma's house. ✔

This is a great way to check your work!

Verb and subjects agree

In a sentence, the subject and the verb **agree**.

The apples **is** on the tree. ✗
The apples **are** on the tree. ✔

The bird **eat** the apple. ✗
The bird **eats** the apple. ✔

The subject of a verb can be in the first, second or third person.

	subject personal pronoun	verb
first person	I	do, play, have
	we	do, play, have
second person	you	do, play, have
third person	he/she/it	does, plays, has
	they	do, play, have

More verb and subject agreements:

She **were** going to the shops. ✗
She **was** going to the shops. ✔

You **was** talking in your sleep last night. ✗
You **were** talking in your sleep last night. ✔

EASY TO REMEMBER

The **subject** personal pronouns are **I, you, he/she/it, we** and **they**.
The **object** personal pronouns are **me, you, him/her/it, us** and **them**.

tenses

Tenses

The verb in a sentence shows the **tense**. It shows when something happens.

The **present** tense shows that something happens now or is true now. It is usually shown by having no ending, or by adding **-s**.

The bird **likes** apples and often **pecks** them to see if they **are** good.

In the third person singular, most verbs have the suffix **-s** in the present tense.

The bird **watches**, and then **flies** across to the tree.

If the verb ends in **-s,-ss**, **-x**, **-sh** or **-ch**, the suffix **-es** is used instead of **-s**.

If the verb ends in consonant + **-y**, the **y** is changed to **i** and then the suffix **-es** is added.

The **progressive** (or continuous) form of the present tense shows that something is in the process of happening now – either happening right now, or continuing over a longer period. It uses the auxiliary verb **be** and the form of the main verb that ends with **-ing**.

What **is** the bird **doing**? It **is pecking** the apple.
This term, Year 6 students **are learning** more about algebra.

-ing form of the main verb

More present progressive:

You **are rushing** to the shops.   She **is walking** to the shops.

The **past** tense is used to describe something that happened earlier. The past tense is normally shown by adding **-ed**.

The bird **pecked** the apple.

*See pages 64 for more on adding **-ed** to verbs.*

More past tenses:

Dad **climbed** the ladder.   We **played** football after school.

WATCH OUT!

See page 66 for more on tricky past tense verbs.

Some verbs change completely in the past tense.

is → was   go → went
think → thought   find → found

The past tense is also used to talk about a situation that is imagined or wished for.

If we **left** now, we'd be able to watch the match on TV. I wish I **had** a dog.

The **progressive** (or continuous) form of the past tense shows that something was in the process of happening – it was not finished, or was still happening when something else happened.

I **was going** to the shops when I lost my glove.

auxiliary verb **be**   **-ing** form of the main verb

tenses

The **perfect** form is used to talk about something that happened, or started happening, earlier. It often shows that something is still relevant, or that something has not stopped happening.

The **present perfect** uses **have** or **has** and the **past participle** of the main verb to show that something is still relevant now.

Jade and Jack **have finished** their work. (So now they can choose a reward.)

> past participle of 'finish'

Jasmine **has** always **wanted** a dog. (This means that she still wants a dog.)

> past participle of 'want'

The **past perfect** uses **had** and a past participle to show that something happened earlier, or was still relevant.

She **had** just **started** her tea when we arrived.

> past participle of 'start'

WATCH OUT!

To make the past participle, you add -ed to most verbs, but not all!
Here are some verbs that change completely:
bite → bitten   break → broken   forget → forgotten
hide → hidden   speak → spoken

WATCH OUT!

The tense is shown by the verb. It is important to use the correct form.
✗ I **visit** my auntie yesterday.
✔ I **visited** my auntie yesterday.

The **future** can be shown by using **will**, or another modal verb, before the main verb.

The bird **will eat** the apple.

> **Will** is the auxiliary (helping) verb and **eat** is the main verb.

The bird **might eat** the apple

> **Might** is the modal verb.

The future can also be shown by using another verb that shows you intend or want something.

The bird **Is going to** eat the apple.   The bird **wants** to eat the apple.

More examples:

We **will be** in France tomorrow.   Dad **will take** me swimming.

WATCH OUT!

Sometimes the main verb is in the present tense, but is about something that will happen in the future.

Rachel **is staying** here tomorrow night.

Active and passive voice

Many verbs can be either active or passive.

This sentence has an active verb:

The little girl **caught** the ball.

In this sentence, the subject of the verb is the little girl – the person who did the action.

active verb

More active sentences:

The bird ate the apple.   The cat chased the bird.

These sentences have a passive verb:

The ball **was caught**.

In these sentences, the subject of the verb is the ball – the thing that had something done to it.

The ball **was caught** by the little girl.

passive verb

In the sentences with a passive verb, the 'do-er' – the little girl – has disappeared, or is mentioned after 'by'.

active and passive voice

The passive voice is useful when it is not known who did the action.

The passive is often used to help build suspense, or to emphasize what happened rather than who did something.

All the cakes had been eaten. *Passive*

The bird had eaten everything! *Active*

Passive verb forms often end in **-ed**, but this does not always mean that they are past tense.

Last year, matches **were played** on Wednesdays.
This year matches **are played** on Sundays.
Next year, matches **will be played** on Fridays.

Grammar in action

A text has **cohesion** if it is clear how its different parts fit together. To do this:

★ Group sentences together in paragraphs.
★ Use words and phrases to link ideas.
★ Repeat key words and phrases in different paragraphs.

A **paragraph** is a group of sentences that are written together. The sentences are usually about the same thing. Start a new paragraph when you are writing about a new idea, person, place or event.

WATCH OUT!

Using the correct verb form or auxiliary is important for cohesion.

Jake wanted to go out. He **had finished** his homework so he thought his mum **would** agree.

shows that Mum had not yet been asked

shows the homework was already done

Grammar

The words and phrases that link ideas in a text are called **cohesive devices**. Here are some examples:

★ Use determiners and pronouns to link back to other words:

Mr Smith came in with his dog. **The** dog and **he** were both old.

> **'The dog'** refers to 'his dog'.

> **'He'** refers to Mr Smith.

★ Use a conjunction to link words or groups of words within a sentence.

★ Use adverbs and adverbials to link between sentences.

Conjunctions, adverbs and adverbials can show different types of connections such as time, place or a reason.

Later, not far away, I saw a green bird. I stopped, **because** I didn't want to scare it.

> links to a previously mentioned time

> links to a previously mentioned place

> links to a reason

More adverbs and adverbials that link ideas to a previous sentence:

moreover   nevertheless   finally   furthermore
therefore   on the other hand   in other words

Ellipsis is when we miss out a word or words because it is obvious what is meant.

For the punctuation mark ellipsis, see page 50

We're off to the park. I can post your letter.

> ellipsis: 'on the way to the park'

31

cohesion

The Olympic Games

Heading – tells you what the writing is about.

In the beginning

The first Olympic Games took place in Ancient Greece about 776BC. They were held in an area called Olympia. There was only one event in **the first Games:** a short running race from one end of the stadium to the other. **Later,** more events were added, such as chariot racing.

Subheading – tells you what the next paragraph or paragraphs are about.

Adverbial – links ideas within paragraphs.

Originally, women and girls were not allowed to take part in the Olympic Games. **As a consequence,** a separate event, called the Herannic Games after the goddess Hera, was held for women to compete in. Like the Olympic Games, women competed in running races. **They** wore short dresses, called chitons. **However,** men competing in the Olympic Games wore no clothes at all.

Pronoun – makes links with the women in the previous sentence.

Adverb acting as a **cohesive device** – links ideas within the paragraph.

The modern Games

Hundreds of years later, the modern Olympic Games began in the nineteenth century, with the foundation of the International Olympic Committee (IOC). The first modern Games were held in Athens in 1896.

Fronted adverbial – answers the question 'When?' and links ideas across paragraphs.

Adverbial – links ideas across paragraphs.

In contrast to the first Olympic Games, the Games now have many events. Men and women compete in the Games, but there are only a few events where they compete against each other.

Repeated phrase – links ideas across paragraphs.

See page 20 for more on adverbials.

Formal and informal language

Formal language is the language we use in official, or formal, situations.

We can use formal language for:
* school work
* debating
* giving a speech
* official forms, letters and emails

In formal language:
* Use formal vocabulary that you do not use in everyday situations.
* Try to use fewer contractions – these are when two words are used as one and an apostrophe shows the missing letters, such as I've and 'they've'.
* Do not use capital letters for emphasis.
* Use Standard English.

Informal language is the language we use in everyday situations.

We can use informal language for:
* ordinary conversation
* letters, emails, texts and messages to family and friends
* notes
* shopping and to-do lists

Informal language may include:
* contractions
* question tags
* capital letters for emphasis and lots of exclamation marks

Grammar

Formal and informal language

Mr V Frankenstein,
Frankenstein Castle,
Switzerland

> In a formal letter write *Dear* and then someone's title (e.g. Mr) and surname or full name (e.g. Frankenstein).

~~Hi Victor~~ Dear Mr Frankenstein,

> Contractions are used mainly in informal writing.

~~I'd~~ I would like to apply for the job of ~~lab~~

> *Lab* is an informal word for *laboratory*.

laboratory assistant ~~saw it in the paper~~ which

was advertised in the newspaper. ~~I've got tons~~

> *Tons* is an informal word that means 'a lot'.

I have a great deal of experience in this ~~kinda~~

~~thing~~ type of work. I note your requirement

that applicants be experienced. ~~I'd love to~~

> Here, the forms **be** and **were** are subjunctives. Subjunctive forms can be used in formal language to show that something must or should happen. They can also show that something is unlikely or uncertain.

~~work at your place~~. If I were able to take up a

position with you and I would be diligent and

> This is not a complete sentence.

punctual. ~~See my cv~~. Please see the enclosed

> Exclamation marks are not often used in formal writing.

cv. ~~Should be fun!~~ I look forward to working

with you. ~~Cheers~~ Yours sincerely, Fritz Klein

> To finish a formal letter use:
> • **Yours sincerely**, if the letter starts with Dear + the person's name
> • **Yours faithfully**, if the letter starts with Dear Sir/Madam.

EASY TO REMEMBER

★ A **question tag** is a short question on the end of a sentence, used when you want someone to respond to what you have said, e.g. He's a teacher, **isn't he**?

Informal email

Hey you!

How's it going? It's been such a SCORCHER today, hasn't it? Bring your cozzie and we'll head for the beach.

Byeeee

Jane

This contraction joins two words, *how* and *is*.

How's it going is more formally written as *How are you?*

Capital letters emphasize how hot it is.

Question tag

Cozzie is an informal word for swimming costume.

Head for means 'go to'.

Repetition of the letter **e** mimics how it might be said in speech.

Standard and non-Standard English

Standard English is used in most books, newspapers and formal documents. In your schoolwork, you should generally use Standard English. Standard English is also used when speaking formally, for example in speeches or meetings. It can be spoken in different accents, e.g. a West Midlands accent or a Welsh accent.

Non-Standard English is mostly used in speech so it can be used when writing down what someone has said. It can also be used in informal writing.

Here are some differences between Standard and non-Standard English:

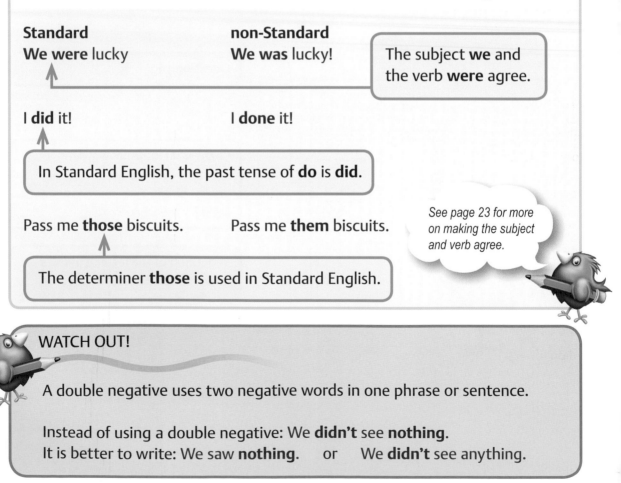

Standard	non-Standard
We were lucky	**We was** lucky!

The subject **we** and the verb **were** agree.

I **did** it!	I **done** it!

In Standard English, the past tense of **do** is **did**.

Pass me **those** biscuits.	Pass me **them** biscuits.

The determiner **those** is used in Standard English.

See page 23 for more on making the subject and verb agree.

WATCH OUT!

A double negative uses two negative words in one phrase or sentence.

Instead of using a double negative: We **didn't** see **nothing**.
It is better to write: We saw **nothing**.   or   We **didn't** see anything.

Grammar

In this extract, Mrs Sweet uses Standard English. Her speech is not formal: she uses a question tag, and the contractions **what's** and **who's**.

Little Paul often uses non-Standard English. Whenever this happens, the Standard English equivalent is shown.

"Now," said Mrs Sweet, "an hour ago there were twelve raspberry buns on the table, and now there are eleven, aren't there? Does anyone have anything to say?"

Mrs Sweet surveyed the group.

"You! You look guilty," she declared, her eyes coming to rest on Little Paul. "Do you want to tell me anything?"

"No, Mrs Sweet, I promise – it weren't me!" Little Paul looked pinker than the jam that oozed from the remaining buns. "I seen them buns, and I thought they was delicious! I mean I thought they looked delicious..."

"He weren't gonna eat it!" burst out the little girl next to him, also turning raspberry pink. "It were for Uncle Paul – as a present."

"Who's Uncle Paul?" enquired Mrs Sweet.

"Me dad," said Little Paul. "I'm sorry, Mrs Sweet. I done it. I didn't have no presents for his birthday, and I seen the buns, and I thought they was fantastic. So I took one. Look – here it is." Out of his bag he took a paper towel, and he unwrapped it carefully to reveal the missing bun. "I didn't take nothing else, though."

It wasn't me

saw

those buns

they were

He wasn't

going to

it was

My dad

I did

I didn't have any presents

I saw

they were

I didn't take anything

37

Good writing

Good writing uses words and language effectively. Here are some things to think about when you are writing:

Be clear

It is important to make your meaning clear. Sometimes, this means being **concise** – using one word instead of several, or fewer words instead of more.

Instead of saying:
I must **get in touch** with my family **straight away**.

You could write:
I must **contact** my family **immediately**.

Be specific

Sometimes it can help the reader to 'see' what you are writing about if you use **specific** rather than general words.

★ For example, *flower* is a general word, but *rose*, *daffodil* and *tulip* are more specific because they describe types of flower.

Instead of saying:
The garden was full of **flowers**.

You could write:
The garden was full of bright **lilies** and sweet **roses**.

Add variety

Synonyms are words that mean the same – or nearly the same – as each other, such as *big* and *huge*, or *horrible* and *nasty*.

Instead of saying that someone ate a whole pizza, you could write:
He **wolfed down** a whole pizza! or He **polished off** a whole pizza!

Instead of saying that someone lived in a big house, you could write:
They lived in an **enormous** house.

★ Sometimes you can choose between a few synonyms. A giant's nose might be *huge* or *immense* or *colossal* – you can swap the words around and it makes no difference to the meaning.

★ At other times you may need to think more carefully about which synonym to use. For example, some are more formal than others:

In a piece of school work, you might write:
The cake was **delicious**.

In your diary or in an email to a friend, you might write:
The cake was **yummy**.

synonyms

Words such as *bad*, *big*, *good* and *nice* can be useful, but you can make your writing more interesting by choosing **unusual** synonyms sometimes.

★ Instead of making a fairy **pretty** or **beautiful**, try describing her as **radiant**.

★ Is a **big ogre** big enough? If not, transform it into a **monstrous ogre**.

Before choosing an alternative word, check that it has the right meaning for your sentence.

★ A **nice person** could mean a **friendly** person, a **kind** person or a **thoughtful** person
BUT
★ **nice weather** doesn't mean the same thing!

Antonyms are words that mean the opposite of each other, such as *wet* and *dry*, *full* and *empty*, *open* and *closed*. See how the antonyms below make sentences with very different meanings.

In the 100m sprint, Jess got off to a **quick** start.

In the 100m sprint, Jess got off to a **slow** start.

Using opposites can be effective in writing:

You think mushrooms are **delicious**? I think they're **revolting**!

EASY TO REMEMBER

You can change the meaning of many words by adding the prefixes **un-**, **in-** and **dis-**.

certain **un**certain   correct **in**correct   agree **dis**agree

WATCH OUT!

Words can also change their meaning completely by adding the suffixes **-ful** and **-less**.

hope**ful**   hope**less**

care**ful**   care**less**

power**ful**   power**less**

See pages 70-79 for more on prefixes and suffixes.

Punctuation

Punctuation marks are used in sentences to make the meaning clear. Sentences can mean very different things if they don't have punctuation.

> Let's eat Granny!
>
> Let's eat, Granny!

Punctuation marks

A **full stop** $\boxed{.}$ comes at the end of a sentence. It shows that a sentence is complete and finished.

It is a full sentence.   I am the tallest in my class.

I like swimming.

More full stops:

Let's go to the park.   We are having lunch now.

You can text me later.

Punctuation

> **Capital letters** are used at the beginning of sentences.
>
> The bird likes to eat seeds.

Capital letters are used for proper nouns (nouns that identify a particular person, place or thing):

* people, e.g. Jacqueline Wilson, Jack, Lucy

* computer games, e.g. Solve it!, MoshiMonsters, Deadly Dash

* brands, e.g. Ferrari, Apple, Samsung

* plays and musicals, e.g. *Macbeth*, *War Horse*, *Matilda*

* places, e.g. London, New York, Mumbai, Park Street

* films, e.g. Shrek, The Lion King, Madagascar

* books, e.g. *War Horse*, *Charlie and the Chocolate Factory*, *Stop the Train!*

* paintings and sculptures, e.g. The Mona Lisa, Campbell's Soup Cans, The Scream, David, The Angel of the North

WATCH OUT!

Always use a capital letter when you use **I** to talk about yourself.

I raised £100 for charity!   All **I**'ve ever wanted was a puppy.   **I**'m cold.

The names of days and months are proper nouns, so they also start with a capital letter.

Monday	Tuesday	Wednesday	Thursday	Friday	Saturday	Sunday

January	February	March	April	May	June
July	August	September	October	November	December

43

Punctuation

A **question mark** (**?**) comes at the end of a sentence which is asking a question.

Where are you**?**

What is your favourite colour**?**

Who was that**?**

Do you like peas**?**

More question marks:

Are you coming to the cinema with us?

How are you?

What time is it?

How old are you?

An **exclamation mark** (**!**) comes at the end of an exclamation. It shows that something is being exclaimed, or said with a lot of feeling.

I'm so late**!**   Hurrah**!**   It's a goal**!**   No**!**

An **exclamation mark** can also come at the end of a command. A command is a sentence which gives an order or instruction.

No**!**   Run**!**

Sit on the blue chair**!**

Stop it**!**

A **comma** (**,**) can be used to separate items in a list.

I like to eat apples, seeds, grapes and nuts.

Punctuation

More commas:

I like peas, carrots, beans and pizza.   I have a sister, a brother and a stepsister.

WATCH OUT!

I ate an orange, an apple, and raspberries.

This is called a serial, or Oxford, comma. In some texts, this is used throughout as a style.

A **comma** (**,**) can be used to change the meaning of a sentence.

I told him, honestly.   I told him honestly.

A **comma** (**,**) can be used to avoid ambiguity.

I'd like some jelly and ice cream for my sister.

This sentence is ambiguous: it is not clear if both the jelly and the ice cream are for the sister.

I'd like some jelly, and ice cream for my sister.

The comma makes it clear that the sister is only having ice cream.

commas

A **comma** (**,**) can be used before a clause starting with **or**, **and** or **but**.

I like swimming, but I love ice skating!

More commas:

Did you paint this picture yourself, **or** did someone help you?

We're finishing dinner, **and** then we're going to play a game.

I like cats, **but** I love dogs!

A **comma** (**,**) is used after a subordinate clause at the start of a sentence.

If we're really quiet, we won't disturb Grandad.

A **comma** (**,**) is also used after a fronted adverbial.

With a shake, the dog dried itself off.   Luckily, I got out of the way in time!!

When Y6 came back from their trip, they were exhausted.

A **comma** (**,**) is used to separate the name of the person being spoken to from the rest of the sentence.

Kids, dinner's ready!   If you want, **Mum**, I'll wash up.

Punctuation

A **colon** : can be used to introduce a list.

I love the following foods: apples, seeds, grapes and nuts.

More colons:

There are three friends in the book: Harry, Ron and Hermione.

We are going to need: knives, forks, spoons and glasses.

They come in four colours: red, blue, yellow and green.

A **colon** : can be used to introduce examples or explanations.

The words after the colon give more information about what comes before it.

The bird eats lots of snacks: he needs lots of energy for flying.

More colons:

It is a big house: there are six bedrooms all with their own bathrooms.

The rabbits are very furry: they need to keep warm in winter.

My favourite colour is blue: it is the colour of my favourite team.

WATCH OUT!

See page 9 for more on nouns.

You don't need to use a capital letter for the word that comes after a colon, unless it is a proper noun or the word 'I'.

semicolons

A **semicolon** (;) can be used between two main clauses. (A main clause can work on its own in a sentence.)

The film was brilliant; I had a great time.

The room is hot; there are a lot of people dancing.

A **semicolon** (;) can be used in lists.

A semicolon can separate longer phrases in a list that has been introduced by a colon, or which is more complicated than a simple list of words.

The children need to bring with them: a hot-water bottle or an extra blanket if the weather is cold; a cup, a plate and a bowl; a knife, a fork and a spoon.

More semicolons:

I need yoghurt; as many bananas as you have; a tub of vanilla ice cream; and chocolate to sprinkle on top.

We all brought four things: a spooky ghost outfit; a funny clown costume; an animal suit; and a loud horn.

WATCH OUT!

Do not use a comma to join sentences or main clauses. If you want to join sentences using punctuation, choose a semicolon, a colon or, if you are writing informally, a dash.

Punctuation

A **dash** (—) can introduce further information and can be used instead of a colon or a comma. After the dash, there may be a list or a main or subordinate clause.

The fire spread quickly and the trees were engulfed — I was scared.

More dashes:

All the dogs were the same — white with black spots.

Everyone needs to work hard — especially if they don't want any extra homework!

Brackets ( ) **commas** (,) and **dashes** (—) can all be used to separate a word or phrase that has been added to a sentence as an explanation or afterthought.

The word or phrase inside the brackets, commas or dashes is called a **parenthesis**.

I looked up, squinting because of the sun, and saw the birds flying across the sky.

If you take out the word or phrase between the two commas, the sentence should still make sense on its own.

More brackets and dashes:

My birthday cake was chocolate (which is my absolute favourite) with chocolate icing and chocolate buttons on top as well.

We catch the bus — the blue one — at 3.15 p.m. at the station.

Punctuation

Ellipsis (...) is used to show that a word has been missed out or a sentence is not finished.

Don't tell me...

A **hyphen** (-) is used to join two or more words that should be read as a single unit. A hyphen is shorter than a dash.

great-aunt   fair-haired

A **hyphen** (-) is also used to help avoid confusion.

a man eating fish   a man-eating fish

This could be a man eating a fish.

This is a fish that eats men.

A **hyphen** (-) is sometimes used between a prefix and a root word, especially if the hyphen makes the word easier to read.

co-ordinate   co-own   re-educate

More hyphens:

a mix-up   a bad-tempered pet

a nine-year-old boy   I re-addressed the envelope.

Punctuation

Inverted commas, or speech marks, " " and ' ' show when people are actually speaking. When people's exact words are written down in this way, this is called **direct speech**.

"I'm beginning to understand," he said.

"Finally!" she replied.

More inverted commas:

"We're too late," I said.　　　　"Can we meet up tomorrow?" Sarah asked.

"We're going swimming later," Dad reminded me.

WATCH OUT!

The punctuation at the end of the spoken words always comes **inside** the final set of inverted commas.

"I can't hold on any longer!" Alex cried. ✔
"I can't hold on any longer"! Alex cried. ✘

'Can I talk to you please?' she whispered. ✔
'Can I talk to you please'? she whispered. ✘

EASY TO REMEMBER

You may see single (' ') or double (" ") inverted commas, depending on what you are reading. It is important to use the same style across your work so that you are consistent.

apostrophes

An **apostrophe** (**'**) can be used to show that letters are missed out of a word (a contraction).

I am sure I didn't pick up the pen.

The two words **did** and **not** are joined and the apostrophe replaces the letter **o** in **not**.

He'd already eaten his dinner.

More than one letter is missing as **he had** is now **he'd** — the apostrophe is instead of more than one letter.

More apostrophes:

it + is = it's
we + are = we're
it + has = it's
does + not = doesn't
do + not = don't
should + not = shouldn't
who + is = who's

had + not = hadn't
would + have = would've
could + not = couldn't
could + have = could've
you + are = you're
he + had = he'd
she + would = she'd

WATCH OUT!

It is easy to confuse **its** and **it's**. If you can say 'it is' or 'it has' instead of 'its' in your sentence, then you should use an apostrophe.

It is raining. = It's raining. ✔   It has finished. = It's finished. ✔
The dog wagged its tail. = The dog wagged it's tail. ✘

Punctuation

An **apostrophe** (**'**) can show ownership or possession.

This is called a **possessive apostrophe**. Possessive apostrophes show that something belongs to, or is for, someone or something. Often, a **possessive apostrophe** is used with a **possessive s**.

★ If a singular word doesn't end in **-s**, add **'s**:
   the boy's pen

possessive apostrophe

★ If a singular word ends in **-s**, add either **'s** or just **'**:
   James's hat   Nicholas' hat

★ If a singular word ends in **-ss**, still add **'s**:
   the princess's crown   the boss's chair
   the witness's statement

★ If a plural ends in **-s**, just add **'**:
   the girls' bags   the visitors' car park   the calves' horns

plural -s before apostrophe

★ If a plural doesn't end in **-s**, add **'s**:
   children's books   men's coats
   women's shoes   mice's food

WATCH OUT!

Adding an apostrophe does not make a word plural!

Cauliflowers are half price! ✔
Cauliflower's are half price! ✗

Bullet points (•) are used to organize a list of points in order to make it clear. The text introducing the list of bullet points should end with a colon.

If the text that follows the bullet point is not a proper sentence, it does not need to start with a capital letter and end with a full stop.

Plan for the holidays:
- finish book
- mend bike
- tidy room

If the text that follows the bullet point is a full sentence, it should start with a capital letter and end with a full stop.

	We gave the following reasons for wanting
	to have a party:
	• It was our last year in primary school.
	• We wanted to say goodbye to our teachers.
	• We had worked hard all year.

WATCH OUT!

Paragraph breaks are also an important part of punctuation.

✗ "Would you like some cake?" asked Sarah. "Yes, please!"

This means that Sarah is talking to herself.

✔ "Would you like some cake?" asked Sarah.

"Yes, please!"

The paragraph break shows that someone else is now speaking.

Spelling

Spelling can be tricky! Think of the word you are spelling and how it sounds. To help you to spell it correctly, here are some spelling rules and strategies.

Vowels and consonants

The letters **a**, **e**, **i**, **o** and **u** are called **vowel letters**. They are in most words. They can make a short vowel sound or a long vowel sound. All other letters are called **consonant letters**.

Vowel letters are a, e, i, o, u.

How to spell the long vowel sounds

a — **/eɪ/ sounds like 'play'**

Different ways of spelling this sound.

ay	day	play
ai	wait	rain
a_e	cake	same
a	acorn	angel
-ae	sundae	
-ey	grey	they
ea	great	break

WATCH OUT!

Other letter groups can also make the /eɪ/ sound: the **eigh** in **eight** and **neighbour** and the **ei** in **vein**.
The **ae** in **ice cream sundae** is an unusual spelling of the /eɪ/ sound.

vowel sounds

e /iː/ sounds like 'tree'

Different ways of spelling this sound:

ee	sweet	peel
e_e	compete	theme
ey	monkey	keys
ie	thief	field
ea	meat	deal
i_e	sardine	

ea can also make the sound in **bread** and **feather**.

WATCH OUT!

At the end of a word, the letter y often makes a sound that is very similar to the long /iː/ sound.

baby   tummy   silly   happy

i /aɪ/ sounds like 'high'

Different ways of spelling this sound:

ie	lie	pie	tie
i_e	kite	despite	alike
igh	light	bright	fright
i	behind	mind	

WATCH OUT!

At the end of a word, the commonest way of spelling the long /aɪ/ sound is the letter **y**.

my   by   fly

For words like gym and mystery that have an 'i' sound in the middle, see page 91.

In height, **ei** makes this sound.

Spelling

o | /əʊ/ sounds like 'road'

Different ways of spelling this sound:

o	so	go
oa	boat	toast
o_e	broke	hole
oe	woe	toe
ow	tow	glow
ough	although	dough
eau	gateau	

Lots of words are spelt with the letters -ough. Have a look at page 86 for the different sounds they can make.

u | /u:/ sounds like 'moon'

Different ways of spelling this sound:

ue	clue	true
u_e	flute	rude
oo	cool	spoon
ew	crew	flew
o	to	who
ou	you	soup
ough	through	
ui	bruise	fruit
u	super	

vowel sounds

y — /ju:/ sounds like 'tube'

Different ways of spelling this sound:

ue	arg**ue**
ew	kn**ew**
u	**u**niverse t**u**na
u_e	c**u**b**e**
eu	f**eu**d

> **You** is spelt with **ou**.

More vowel sounds

sound	examples					
short 'oo'	book	could	push			
'ar'	car	father	palm			
'or'	fork	saw	your	saucer	oar	floor
	more	war	reward	toward	naughty	brought
	warm	quarter	water	walk	all	
'ur'	burn	her	bird	early	word	
'ou'	clown	found	plough			
'oi'	coin	toy				
'eer'	hear	sphere	pier	deer		
'air'	chair	care	bear	there		
'yoor'	cure					

WATCH OUT!

The 'ur' sound in **ear**n, **lear**n, h**ear**d and **ear**ly is spelt with the letter group **ear**.

The 'air' sound in teddy b**ear** is spelt with the letter group **ear**.

Making nouns plural

A noun names a person or thing. Words like apple, dog, team and chair are all nouns. One apple is **singular**. More than one is **plural**.

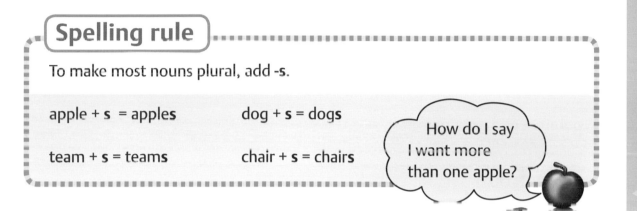

┌─ **Spelling rule** ─┐

To make most nouns plural, add **-s**.

apple + **s** = apple**s**   dog + **s** = dog**s**

team + **s** = team**s**   chair + **s** = chair**s**

How do I say I want more than one apple?

The little bird has one **apple** on his head.

There are lots of **apples** on the ground.

Now think about...

If the noun ends in **-s**, **-ss**, **-x**, **-sh** or **-ch**, add **-es**.

bus + **es** = bus**es**   glass + **es** = glass**es**   fox + **es** = fox**es**

brush + **es** = brush**es**   church + **es** = church**es**

If the noun ends in a consonant + **-y**, change the **-y** to **-i** and add **-es**.

bab~~y~~ → **ie** + s = bab**ies**   bod~~y~~ → **ie** + s = bod**ies**   famil~~y~~ → **ie** + s = famil**ies**

If the noun ends in **-f** or **-fe**, change the **-f** or **-fe** to **-ves**.

half + **ves** = hal**ves**   life + **ves** = li**ves**

If the noun ends in **-o**, add **-es**.

hero + **es** = hero**es**   tomato + **es** = tomato**es**

potato + **es** = potato**es**

WATCH OUT!

Some nouns ending in **-f** and **-o** only need an **-s** to make the plural!

roof + **s** = roof**s**

piano + **s** = piano**s**

Some plurals do not add '-s'

> For some nouns that ends in **-a**, add an **-e**.
>
> antenna + **e** = antenna**e**

> For some nouns that ends in **-us**, change the **-us** to an **i**.
>
> fung~~us~~ → **i** = fung**i**

> If the noun ends in **-is**, change the **-is** to **-es**.
>
> cris~~is~~ → **es** = cris**es**

> There are some tricky nouns that do not change at all to make the plural.
>
> one **sheep** → two **sheep**   one **deer** → two **deer**

> Some words change their spelling completely to make the plural.
>
> child → **children**   mouse → **mice**
>
> man → **men**

Adding -ing to verbs to make present participles

A verb often (but not always) names an action. Words like pick, jump, fly and mix are all verbs.

> I am pick**ing** up my apples.

Spelling rule

Progressive forms of verbs use present participles. To make a present participle, add **-ing** to the verb.

rain + **ing** = rain**ing**   rush + **ing** = rush**ing**

laugh = **ing** = laugh**ing**

See page 24 for more on tenses.

Now think about...

If a verb ends in consonant + **-e**, take off the **-e** and add **-ing**.

juggle + **ing** = juggl**ing**   tickle + **ing** = tickl**ing**

More examples:

shine + **ing** = shin**ing**   race + **ing** = rac**ing**   smile + **ing** = smil**ing**

WATCH OUT!

be + **-ing** = be**ing**

If a verb ends in a single vowel letter and a single consonant letter, double the consonant and add **-ing**.

trip + **p** + **ing** = trip**ping**   shop + **p** + **ing** = shop**ping**

More examples:

hop + **p** + **ing** = hop**ping**   rub + **b** + **ing** = rub**bing**

swim + **m** + **ing** = swim**ming**

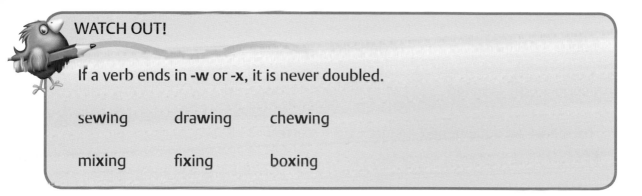

WATCH OUT!

If a verb ends in **-w** or **-x**, it is never doubled.

sewing   drawing   chewing

mixing   fixing   boxing

If a verb ends in **-y**, just add **-ing**.

cry + **ing** = cry**ing**   fly + **ing** = fly**ing**   reply + **ing** = reply**ing**

copy + **ing** = copy**ing**   carry + **ing** = carry**ing**   stay + **ing** = stay**ing**

If a verb ends in **-ie**, change the **-ie** to **-y** before adding **-ing**.

tie → **y** = t**y**ing   lie → **y** = l**y**ing   die → **y** = d**y**ing

Adding -ed to verbs to make a past tense

I pick**ed** a juicy apple!

Spelling rule

To make a past tense or past participle, add **-ed** to the verb.

pick + **ed** = pick**ed**   weigh + **ed** = weigh**ed**

laugh + **ed** = laugh**ed**   whisper + **ed** = whisper**ed**

happen + **ed** = happen**ed**   start + **ed** = start**ed**

WATCH OUT!

Many common verbs do not form their past tense or past participle in this way. See pages 66 and 67 for more information.

Now think about...

If a verb ends in a consonant + **-e**, take off the **-e** and add **-ed**.

smil~~e~~ + **ed** = smil**ed**   hik~~e~~ + **ed** = hik**ed**

pok~~e~~ + **ed** = pok**ed**   tickl~~e~~ + **ed** = tickl**ed**

If a verb ends in a single vowel letter and a single consonant letter, double the consonant and add **-ed**.

clap+ **p** + **ed** = clap**ped**   pat + **t** + **ed** = pat**ted**

tap + **p** + **ed** = tap**ped**

If a verb ends in a consonant + **-y**, change the **-y** to **-i** and add **-ed**.

cry → **i** + **ed** = cr**ied**   try → **i** + **ed** = tr**ied**

copy → **i** + **ed** = cop**ied**   carry → **i** + **ed** = carr**ied**

If a verb ends in a vowel + **-y**, just add **-ed**.

play + **ed** = play**ed**   stay + **ed** = stay**ed**

obey + **ed** = obey**ed**

If a verb ends in **-ie**, take off the e and add **-ed**.

tie + **d** = ti**ed**   lie + **d** = li**ed**

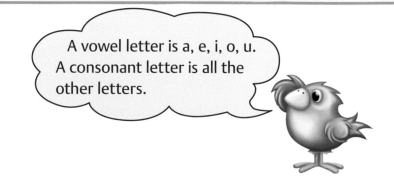

A vowel letter is a, e, i, o, u.
A consonant letter is all the other letters.

irregular verbs

Some verbs change completely to make the past tense and past participle.

verb	past tense	past participle
begin →	began	begun
bend →	bent	bent
bite →	bit	bitten
blow →	blew	blown
break →	broke	broken
buy →	bought	bought
catch →	caught	caught
creep →	crept	crept
dig →	dug	dug
do →	did	done
drink →	drank	drunk
drive →	drove	driven
eat →	ate	eaten
feed →	fed	fed
fight →	fought	fought
find →	found	found
get →	got	got
give →	gave	given
go →	went	gone
grow →	grew	grown
have →	had	had
hear →	heard	heard

verb	past tense	past participle
hide →	hid	hidden
keep →	kept	kept
know →	knew	known
make →	made	made
meet →	met	met
ride →	rode	ridden
ring →	rang	rung
rise →	rose	risen
run →	ran	run
see →	saw	seen
sell →	sold	sold
send →	sent	sent
shake →	shook	shaken
shoot →	shot	shot
sing →	sang	sung
sit →	sat	sat
sleep →	slept	slept
slide →	slid	slid
speak →	spoke	spoken
spend →	spent	spent
sweep →	swept	swept
swim →	swam	swum

Spelling

verb	past tense	past participle
take →	**took**	**taken**
teach →	**taught**	**taught**
tear →	**tore**	**torn**
tell →	**told**	**told**
think →	**thought**	**thought**

verb	past tense	past participle
throw →	**threw**	**thrown**
wear →	**wore**	**worn**
weep →	**wept**	**wept**
wind →	**wound**	**wound**
write →	**wrote**	**written**

WATCH OUT!

There is one verb you need to be extra careful with! The verb **to be** has more than one form both in the present tense and in the past tense.

Past tense

I **was**   we **were**   you **were**   they **were**   he/she/it **was**

Present tense

I **am**   we **are**   you **are**   they **are**   he/she/it **is**

Adding -er and -est to adjectives

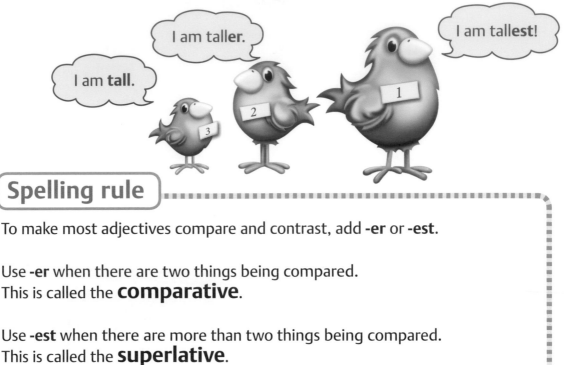

I am **tall**.

I am tall**er**.

I am tall**est!**

1

2

3

Spelling rule

To make most adjectives compare and contrast, add **-er** or **-est**.

Use **-er** when there are two things being compared.
This is called the **comparative**.

Use -**est** when there are more than two things being compared.
This is called the **superlative**.

long	long**er**	long**est**		fast	fast**er**	fast**est**
slow	slow**er**	slow**est**		small	small**er**	small**est**
quick	quick**er**	quick**est**		short	short**er**	short**est**

Now think about...

If an adjective ends in **-e**, take off the **-e** and add **-er** or **-est**.

rude + -**er** / -**est** = rud**er** / rud**est**   nice + -**er** / -**est** = nic**er** / nic**est**

huge + -**er** / -**est** = hug**er** / hug**est**

Spelling

If the adjective ends in a single vowel letter and a single consonant letter, double the consonant and add **-er** or **-est**.

hot + **t** + **-er** / **-est** = hot**ter** / hot**test**

fit + **t** + **er** / **-est** = fit**ter** / fit**test**

big + **g** + **er** / **-est** = big**ger** / big**gest**

If the adjective ends in a consonant + **-y**, change the **-y** to **-i** and add **-er** or **-est**.

funny → **i** + **-er** / **-est** = funn**ier** /funn**iest**

shiny → **i** + **-er** / **-est** – shin**ier** / shin**iest**

wobbly → **i** + **-er** / **-est** = wobb**lier** / wobb**liest**

★ Some two-syllable words can use either **more** or **most**, or **-er** or **-est**.

clever   clever**er** / **more** clever   clever**est** / **most** clever

★ Adjectives with three or more syllables use **more** or **most** instead of adding **-er** or **-est**.

interesting   **more** interesting   **most** interesting

WATCH OUT!

For two-syllable adjectives ending in **-ful**, **-less**, **-ing**, **-ed** and **-ous** use **more** or **most**.

famous   **more** famous   **most** famous
beautiful   **more** beautiful   **most** beautiful

Prefixes

Prefixes are useful!

A **prefix** is a group of letters that can be added to the beginning of a root word.

Different prefixes have different meanings so, when you add a prefix to a word, you change its meaning and make a new word.

dis + appear = **dis**appear   **im** + possible = **im**possible

un + well = **un**well   **sub** + marine = **sub**marine

prefix	meaning	example	
re-	again	recycle	reuse
pre-	before	prehistoric	
ex-	out, outside of	export	exit
co-	together	cooperate	coordinate
anti-	against	antiseptic	anti-hero
auto-	self	automatic	autobiography
circum-	round, about	circumference	
bi-	two, twice	bicycle	
tele-	at a distance	telephone	
trans-	across	transport	transatlantic
pro-	supporting	programme	proceed
sub-	below	submarine	
inter-	between, among	international	
super-	above, over, beyond	superman	supersize
over-	excessively	overused	overexcited

A root word is the most basic form of a word.

prefixes

Some prefixes make the opposite of the word.

prefix	meaning	example	
un-	not, the opposite of	unwell	
de-	undoing or taking away	deflate	
dis-	not	dishonest	
dis-	opposite of	disappear	
mis-	wrong	misbehave	
non-	not	non-stop	
in- / im- / ir- / il-	not	incredible	impossible
		irregular	illegal

WATCH OUT!

The prefix **in-** can mean both 'not' and 'in' or 'into'.

inedible = not edible

Indoors = inside (your house)

Suffixes

A **suffix** is a group of letters that can be added to the end of a root word.

Different suffixes have different meanings so, when you add a suffix to a word, you change its meaning and make a new word.

fast + **er** = fast**er**   sad + **ness** = sad**ness**

joy + **ful** = joy**ful**   hope + **less** = hope**less**

suffix	meaning	example
-er	more	faster
-est	most	fastest
-ible / -able	able to be	possible miserable
-hood	nouns of state or condition	childhood
-ness	nouns of state or condition	kindness

Some suffixes can change a word into a different **word class**.

The word class tells us the job the word does in a sentence, such as a noun or a verb.

teach (verb) + **er** = teach**er** (noun)

apology (noun) + **ize** = apolog**ize** (verb)

quick (adjective) + **ly** = quick**ly** (adverb)

Spelling

EASY TO REMEMBER

-able or **-ible**?

More words end in **-able** than **-ible**. A useful way of checking your spelling is to see if you have a root word left after taking off the **-able**. If not, then the ending is usually **-ible**.

eat~~able~~ = eat ✔ ⟶ eatable ✔

poss~~ible~~ = poss ✘ ⟶ possible ✔

For some words that end in **-y**, take the **-y** away before adding **-able**.
miser~~y~~ + **able** = miser**able**

For other words that end in **-y**, change the **-y** to **-i** before adding **-able**.
env~~y~~ → **i** + **able** = env**i**able

EASY TO REMEMBER

When using **-er** to make a noun, use the same spelling rules as for adding **-er** to adjectives: double a single consonant letter after a single vowel letter:

run + **n** + **er** = run**ner**
swim + **m** + **er** = swim**mer**

If a verb ends in a consonant + -e, take off the -e and add -er.

rid~~e~~ + **er** = rid**er**
strik~~e~~ + **er** = strik**er**

suffixes

These suffixes can be used to change **verbs** into **nouns**.

suffix	meaning	verb	noun
-er	a person or thing that does something	teach	teacher
-or	a person or thing that does something	act	actor
-ment	nouns of action or purpose	enjoy	enjoyment
-ant / -ent	someone who does something	attend	attendant
-tion / -ation	nouns of action or condition	direct inform	direction information

These suffixes can be used to change **nouns** into **verbs**.

suffix	noun	verb
-ate	pollen	pollinate
-ise or -ize	apology	apologise apologize
-ify	note	notify

These suffixes can be used to make **adjectives**.

suffix	meaning	example
-ous	characterized by	dangerous
-ful	full of	playful
-less	not having/without	fearless

WATCH OUT!

The suffix meaning full is **-ful**, with just one l.

Spelling

The suffix **-ly** can be used to change **adjectives** into **adverbs**.

quick + **ly** = quick**ly**   sudden + **ly** =sudden**ly**

If the adjective ends in consonant + **-y**, you usually change the **y** to **i** and then add **-ly**.

happy → **i** + **ly** = happ**ily**   hungry → **i** + **ly** = hungr**ily**

If the adjective ends in **-le**, remove the **-le** before adding **-ly**.

unbelievable + **ly** = unbelievab**ly**

These suffixes can be used to make **adjectives** and **nouns**.

suffix	adjective	noun
-al	historical	arrival
-ary	military	dictionary
-ic	rhythmic	mechanic
-ive	attractive	native

WATCH OUT!

When adding the suffix **-y**, use the same spelling rules as for adding **-er**: double a single consonant letter after a single vowel letter.
sun + **n** + **y** = sun**ny**
spot + **t** + **y** = spot**ty**

If a word ends in a consonant + **-e**, take off the **-e** and add **-y**.
bone + **y** = bony

Spelling suffixes

Spelling rule

The sound 'shun' can be spelt in different ways. The endings you need to choose between are **-ion** and **-ian**. The last letter of the root word tells you to put **t**, **s**, **ss** or **c** in front of these.

For words ending in **-t** or **-te**, use **-tion**.

collect + **tion** = collec**tion**   loca~~te~~ + **tion** = loca**tion**

For words ending in **-ss** or **-mit**, use **-ssion**.

posse~~ss~~ + **ssion** = posse**ssion**   permi~~t~~ + **ssion** = permi**ssion**

For words ending in **-d**, **-de** or **-se**, use **-sion**.

expan~~d~~ + **sion** = expan**sion**   revi~~se~~ + **sion** = revi**sion**

For words ending in **-c** or **-cs**, use **-cian**.

magi~~c~~ + **cian** = magi**cian**   politi~~cs~~ + **cian** = politi**cian**

WATCH OUT!

Exceptions are **intention** and **attention**. The root words are **intend** and **attend** but they add **-tion**.

Spelling

suffixes

EASY TO REMEMBER

If a suffix sounds like 'zhun' then it is always spelt **-sion.**

colli**sion**   televi**sion**   deci**sion**   revi**sion**

Spelling rule

It is not always easy to know whether to use **-ent**, **-ence** or **-ency** or **-ant**, **-ance** or **-ancy.** Here are some tips to help you.

-ent, **-ence** or **-ency** often follow a **soft c**, **soft g** or **qu**.

innoc**ent**   innoc**ence**   intellig**ent**   intellig**ence**

frequ**ent**   frequ**ency**

Use **-ant**, **-ance** or **-ancy** if you know there is a related word that ends in **-ation**.

hesit**ation**   hesit**ant**   hesit**ancy**

toler**ation**   toler**ant**   toler**ance**

observ**ation**   observ**ant**   observ**ance**

EASY TO REMEMBER

Try to think of clever ways to remember the correct ending.

Curr**ent** or curr**ant**? Electric current has an **e**, the other is a currant bun!

suffixes

Spelling rule

The sound 'shul' can be spelt **-cial** or **-tial**. A useful guide is that you often use **-cial** after a vowel. You often use **-tial** after a consonant.

spe**cial**	so**cial**	offi**cial**
essen**tial**	par**tial**	presiden**tial**

WATCH OUT!

Look out! There are lots of exceptions!

finan**cial**   ini**tial**   spa**tial**

Spelling rule

The 'shus' sound can be spelt **-cious** or **-tious**. You usually use **-cious** if the root word ends in **-ce**.

spa**ce** spa**cious**	caution cau**tious**
gra**ce** gra**cious**	infect infec**tious**

Spelling rule

The 'zhuh' sound at the end of a word is spelt **-sure**.

The 'chuh' sound at the end of a word is spelt **-ture**.

trea**sure**	plea**sure**	mea**sure**
pic**ture**	adven**ture**	mix**ture**

WATCH OUT!

Be careful! The 'chuh' sound can also be made by the letter group **-cher** at the end of a word.

tea**cher**	ri**cher**	cat**cher**

Using apostrophes

Apostrophes can show when a word has been made shorter by dropping one or more letters. This is called a **contraction**. You usually use contractions in informal writing or when writing direct speech.

I am = I'm   did not = didn't

could not = couldn't   we are = we're

you have = you've   she will/she shall = she'll

See pages 52 and 53 for more on the apostrophe.

WATCH OUT!

Be careful not to confuse these words!

it's (it is) and its   who's (who is) and whose

you're (you are) and your   we're (we are) and were

plurals

Apostrophes are also used to show when someone or something owns something. For most of these nouns you add an **apostrophe** followed by an **-s**.

Tom**'s** trains

The trains belong to Tom.

EASY TO REMEMBER

BUT when the noun is plural and already ends in **-s** you just add the apostrophe.

The birds**'** apples

The apples belong to both birds.

WATCH OUT!

Some plurals are irregular and do not end with **-s**. For some of these, you need to add an **apostrophe** followed by **-s**.

children + **'s** = children's

The children**'s** playground is closed.

Homophones

> **Homophones** are words that have the same pronunciation but different meanings, origins or spelling.
>
> It is easy to use the wrong homophone. It is important to choose the right word.

My **new** friend.

I **knew** it would be fun having a friend.

Easy to confuse

new	knew		no	know		right	write
through	threw		hole	whole		great	grate
for	four		heard	herd		see	sea
be	bee		blue	blew		bare	bear
one	won		cheap	cheep		night	knight

WATCH OUT!

Be careful not to confuse **their**, **they're** and **there**.

It is **their** house.   **Their** means 'belongs to them'.

They're going to the house.   **They're** means 'they are'.

There is the house.   **There** shows place or position.

Homographs

> **Homographs** are words that are spelt the same but not necessarily pronounced the same and have different meanings and origins.

We are **rowing** a boat.

We are **rowing** about the boat.

Some examples of homographs

| bow | Tie a **bow** in your hair. |
| | Take a **bow** after your performance. |

| tear | There is a **tear** in my eye. |
| | I **tear** the page out of the book. |

| wind | I **wind** my scarf around my neck. |
| | The leaves flutter in the **wind**. |

| rose | My favourite kind of flower is a **rose**. |
| | I **rose** late and had to run to school. |

WATCH OUT!

Some words are not exactly the same but they are still easy to confuse, e.g. **accept** and **except**, and **loose** and **lose**. You can find information about these words in the Dictionary section of this book.

Silent letters

Some words have silent letters in them. There are some rules to help you but it is a good idea to try to learn them.

Spelling rule

Silent **l** can follow vowels **a**, **o** and **ou**.	talk chalk calm half calf salmon yolk folk should would could
Silent **b** can come after m or come before t.	plum**b** dum**b** num**b** bom**b** tom**b** lam**b** thum**b** crum**b** de**b**t dou**b**t
Silent **k** can come before **n**.	**k**now **k**neel **k**not **k**nock **k**night **k**nife **k**nob **k**nickers **k**nit **k**nee **k**nuckle
Silent **g** can come before **n**.	**g**nomes **g**nat **g**naw **g**narled
Silent **n** can follow **m**.	solem**n** colum**n**
Silent **w** can come before **r**.	**w**rite **w**rong **w**rist **w**reck **w**retch **w**rinkle **w**rapper **w**restle
Silent **p** can come before **n**, **s** or **t**.	**p**neumatic **p**salm **p**terosaur
Silent **h** can follow **w**, **r** and **c**.	**wh**eat **wh**ale **wh**ine **wh**irl **wh**en **wh**y **wh**ere **wh**at **rh**ino **ch**emist **ch**ord **rh**ubarb

WATCH OUT!

sword and answer also have a silent **w**

WATCH OUT!

Some words start with a silent **h**.
honest   hour   heir

WATCH OUT!

Silent **t** comes between a single vowel letter and **ch**, in words like **catch**, **fetch** and **pitch**.

Exceptions are **rich**, **much**, **such** and **which** and words where **ch** makes a different sound e.g. **brochure** and **technology**.

More spelling rules

Soft g and soft c

What happens when you add **i**, **e** or **y** to a **g** or a **c**?

The **g** usually becomes a '**j**' sound   The **c** becomes an '**s**' sound.
giraffe **ge**rm **gy**m   **ci**rcus **ce**ntre **cy**cle

How to spell the 'dz' sound at the end of a word

The letter **j** is very rarely seen at the end of a word. If it is straight after a short vowel, the 'dz' sound is nearly always spelt **-dge**.

ba**dge**   he**dge**   bri**dge**   splo**dge**   bu**dge**

Otherwise, at the end of a word it is spelt **-ge**.

ora**nge**   bar**ge**   hu**ge**   stra**nge**   cri**nge**

WATCH OUT!

These words rhyme with **fridge** but end in **-age**.
village   passage   language   garage

How to spell the 'v' sound at the end of a word

The letter **v** is very rarely seen at the end of a word. Words that end with a 'v' sound nearly always end with **-ve**.

gi**ve**   ha**ve**   lo**ve**   mo**ve**

a can sound like 'o'

Usually the letter **a** sounds like 'o' when it has a **w** in front of it.
was   s**wa**mp   **wa**sp   s**wa**llow   **wa**nder   s**wa**t   **wa**nt
s**wa**n   **wa**sh   **wa**tch   **wa**llet

Usually the letter group **ar** sounds like 'or' when it has a **w** in front of it.
war   s**war**m   **war**n   rewar**d**   towar**d**s

The sounds made by the letter group ough

Lots of words are spelt with the letter group **ough**, but they can sound very different from each other. This table shows you the different sounds these letters can make. Some of these words are very common.

the 'or' sound	the 'oa' sound	the 'oo' sound	the 'u' sound	the 'ow' sound	the 'off' sound	the 'uff' sound
ought	th**ough**	thr**ough**	thor**ough**	pl**ough**	c**ough**	r**ough**
b**ough**t	alth**ough**		bor**ough**	b**ough**	tr**ough**	t**ough**
th**ough**t	d**ough**					en**ough**
n**ough**t						

Spelling

y can make an /ɪ/ sound, as in 'myth'

Some words use a letter y to represent the short /ɪ/ sound. You need to learn these words as you come across them. Here are some examples:

gym   mystery   cymbal   system   syllable   typical   rhythm

When **que** and **gue** sound like 'k' and 'g'

-**que** and -**gue** at the end of words can sound like 'k' and 'g'.

anti**que**   uni**que**

dialo**gue**   ton**gue**   lea**gue**

The sounds made by the letter group **ou**

Lots of words are spelt with the letter group **ou**, but they can sound very different from each other. This table shows you the different sounds these letters can make. Lots of these words are ones you use often.

the '**ow**' sound	the '**oo**' sound	the '**or**' sound	the '**u**' sound
out	y**ou**	f**ou**r	y**ou**ng
h**ou**se	gr**ou**p	p**ou**r	d**ou**ble
m**ou**se		y**ou**r	tr**ou**ble
ab**ou**t			c**ou**try

Tricky letters

The letter group **ch** sometimes makes a 'k' sound.

s**ch**ool   **ch**orus   **ch**emist

The letter group **ph** makes an 'f' sound.

phrase   **ph**otogra**ph**

The letter group **ch** sometimes makes a 'sh' sound.

chateau   **ch**ef   bro**ch**ure

The letter group **sc** sometimes makes a 's' sound.

science   **sc**ene   fa**sc**inate

The endings **el**, **le** or **al**

-le is a more common ending than **-el** and **-al**, especially in two-syllable words.

The ending **-le** often comes after a letter with an ascender (**b**, **d**, **k**).
ab**le**   midd**le**   cand**le**   chuck**le**

The ending **-le** is also often preceded by letters with a descender (**y**, **g**).
gig**gle**   an**gle**   sty**le**

The ending **-le** comes after a hard **c** or hard **g** sound:
un**cle**   gig**gle**   an**gle**

The ending **-el** often comes after **m**, **n**, **r**, **s**, **v**, **w** or by a soft **c** or soft **g** sound.
cam**el**   tunn**el**   squirr**el**   tins**el**   trav**el**   tow**el**
par**cel**   ang**el**

The ending **-al** often comes after **d**, **b**, **d** or **t**.
ped**al**   cannib**al**   med**al**   met**al**   pet**al**

Top tips!

If you are unsure of how to spell a word there are tips that can help you.

 1 Segment the word into its individual phonemes – break up the word into its sounds.

2 Clap the syllables of the word.

3 Is it a compound word, a word made up of two words such as play + ground? Split the word up!

4 Make up a mnemonic for a word you find difficult.

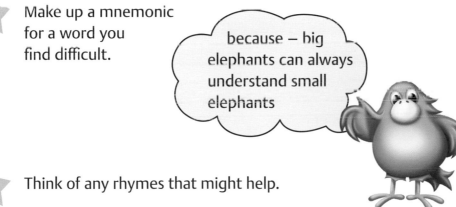

because – big elephants can always understand small elephants

 5 Think of any rhymes that might help.

q is usually followed by **u** (e.g. **qu**een, **qu**iet)

i before **e** except after **c** when the sound is '**ee**' (e.g. bel**ie**ve, dec**ei**ve)

e before **i** is always the way when the sound is '**ay**' (e.g. n**ei**ghbour, w**ei**gh)

6 Remember that many words have unstressed syllables. For instance, if you read the following words aloud, you will notice that in some syllables (the stressed syllables) you can hear the vowel clearly, and in some (the unstressed syllables) you cannot:

sist**er**   hard**er**   teach**er**

phot**o**graph   **o**bserv**a**nt

> Knowing about letter patterns and spelling rules can help with spelling unstressed syllables.

7 Think of word families (related words). Word families are related to each other by spelling, grammar and meaning. When you know how to spell one member of the family, you can use it to help spell other words.

medicine   medicinal
write   writer
noise   noisy   noiseless
extend   extensive
photograph   photographer

Sometimes thinking of other words in a word family can help you to spell a word with an unstressed syllable. For instance, in **medicine** the first i is not always clearly pronounced, but the sound of this letter is clearly heard in **medicinal**.

8 Use the next part of this book, the Spelling dictionary, to look up your word. You will find extra help at the most tricky spellings. This will help you to remember the correct spelling so that you can get it right next time!

How to use this dictionary

alphabet
The alphabet is on every page with the letter you are in highlighted, so you can find your way around the dictionary quickly and easily.

catch words
These are the first and last words on the page, they will guide you to the correct place to find the words you need.

headword
In alphabetical order, it shows you how to spell the word.

try also
This note helps you to check in other parts of the dictionary to find your word.

word class
This is the headword type, for example, noun, verb, adjective or adverb.

asterisk
If the word has a little star next to it, check the footnote for the same star and read the note.

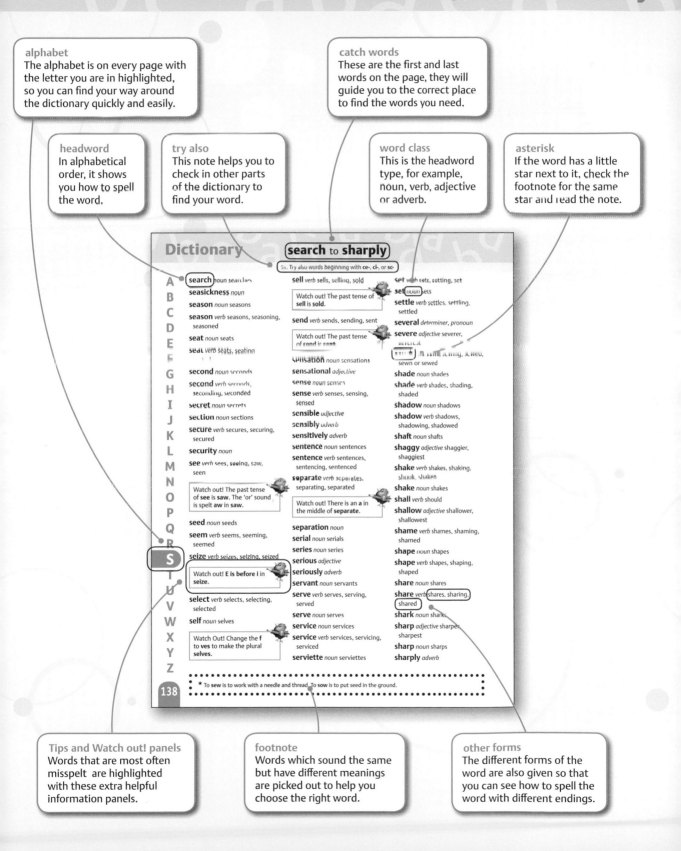

Dictionary

search to sharply

Ss. Try also words beginning with ce-, ci-, or sc-

search noun searches

seasickness noun

season noun seasons

season verb seasons, seasoning, seasoned

seat noun seats

seat verb seats, seating

second noun seconds

second verb seconds, seconding, seconded

secret noun secrets

section noun sections

secure verb secures, securing, secured

security noun

see verb sees, seeing, saw, seen

> Watch out! The past tense of **see** is **saw**. The 'or' sound is spelt **aw** in **saw**.

seed noun seeds

seem verb seems, seeming, seemed

seize verb seizes, seizing, seized

> Watch out! **E** is before **i** in **seize**.

select verb selects, selecting, selected

self noun selves

> Watch Out! Change the **f** to **ves** to make the plural **selves**.

sell verb sells, selling, sold

> Watch out! The past tense of **sell** is **sold**.

send verb sends, sending, sent

> Watch out! The past tense of **send** is **sent**.

sensation noun sensations

sensational adjective

sense noun senses

sense verb senses, sensing, sensed

sensible adjective

sensibly adverb

sensitively adverb

sentence noun sentences

sentence verb sentences, sentencing, sentenced

separate verb separates, separating, separated

> Watch out! There is an **a** in the middle of **separate**.

separation noun

serial noun serials

series noun series

serious adjective

seriously adverb

servant noun servants

serve verb serves, serving, served

serve noun serves

service noun services

service verb services, servicing, serviced

serviette noun serviettes

set verb sets, setting, set

set noun sets

settle verb settles, settling, settled

several determiner, pronoun

severe adjective severer, severest

sew ✱ verb sews, sewing, sewed, sewn or sewed

shade noun shades

shade verb shades, shading, shaded

shadow noun shadows

shadow verb shadows, shadowing, shadowed

shaft noun shafts

shaggy adjective shaggier, shaggiest

shake verb shakes, shaking, shook, shaken

shake noun shakes

shall verb should

shallow adjective shallower, shallowest

shame verb shames, shaming, shamed

shape noun shapes

shape verb shapes, shaping, shaped

share noun shares

share verb shares, sharing, shared

shark noun sharks

sharp adjective sharper, sharpest

sharp noun sharps

sharply adverb

✱ To **sew** is to work with a needle and thread. To **sow** is to put seed in the ground.

138

Tips and Watch out! panels
Words that are most often misspelt are highlighted with these extra helpful information panels.

footnote
Words which sound the same but have different meanings are picked out to help you choose the right word.

other forms
The different forms of the word are also given so that you can see how to spell the word with different endings.

Aa

abandon *verb* abandons, abandoning, abandoned

ability *noun* abilities

able *adjective* abler, ablest

aboard *adverb, preposition*

about *preposition, adverb*

above *preposition, adverb*

abruptly *adverb*

absolute *adjective*

absolutely *adverb*

> Watch Out! Start with **absolute** and add **-ly** to spell **absolutely**.

absorb *verb* absorbs, absorbing, absorbed

accept★ *verb* accepts, accepting, accepted

accident *noun* accidents

accidentally *adverb*

> Watch Out! To make this word from **accident**, add **-ally**.

accommodate *verb* accommodates, accommodating, accommodated

> Double up! There is a double **c** and double **m** in **accommodation**.

accompany *verb* accompanies, accompanying, accompanied

account *noun* accounts

account *verb* accounts, accounting, accounted

ache *noun* aches

ache *verb* aches, aching, ached

across *adverb, preposition*

act *noun* acts

act *verb* acts, acting, acted

action *noun* actions

activity *noun* activities

actually *adverb*

address *noun* addresses

address *verb* addresses, addressing, addressed

> Double up! There is a double **d** and double **s** in **address**.

admiration *noun*

admire *verb* admires, admiring, admired

admission *noun* admissions

adopt *verb* adopts, adopting, adopted

adorable *adjective*

adoration *noun*

adult *noun* adults

advance *noun* advances

advance *verb* advances, advancing, advanced

advantage *noun* advantages

adventure *noun* adventures

advertise *verb* advertises, advertising, advertised

advice *noun*

advise *verb* advises, advising, advised

> Choose the right spelling! **Advice** is a noun and **advise** is a verb, e.g. *a word of advice* and *I advise you to forget the whole thing.*

affair *noun* affairs

affect✪ *verb* affects, affecting, affected

affection *noun* affections

afford *verb* affords, affording, afforded

afraid *adjective*

after *preposition, adverb*

afternoon *noun* afternoons

again *adverb*

> Watch out! **Again** is spelt **a** + **gain** = **again**.

against *preposition*

age *noun* ages

age *verb* ages, ageing, aged

agent *noun* agents

ago *adverb*

agree *verb* agrees, agreeing, agreed

ahead *adverb*

aid *noun* aids

aid *verb* aids, aiding, aided

air *noun* airs

air *verb* airs, airing, aired

aisle☆ *noun* aisles

alarm *verb* alarms, alarming, alarmed

★ **Accept** is different from **except**: to **accept** something is to take it; **except** means not including.
✪ **Affect** means to make something change. An **effect** (noun) is something that is caused by something else.
☆ An **aisle** is a passage in a church or cinema. An **isle** is an island.

a b c d e f g h i j k l m n o p q r s t u v w x y z

A
B
C
D
E
F
G
H
I
J
K
L
M
N
O
P
Q
R
S
T
U
V
W
X
Y
Z

alarm *noun* alarms

alive *adjective*

all *determiner, adverb, pronoun*

all right *adjective, interjection*

> Watch out! **All right** is two words.

allow★ *verb* allows, allowing, allowed

> **Allowed** means to be permitted to do something. **Aloud** means in a voice that can be heard. *He read the letter aloud. Running in the corridors is not allowed.*

almost *adverb*

alone *adjective, adverb*

along *preposition, adverb*

alongside *preposition, adverb*

aloud★ *adverb*

alphabet *noun* alphabets

already *adverb*

also *adverb*

altar✪ *noun* altars

alter✪ *verb* alters, altering, altered

although *conjunction*

> Watch out! There is only one **l** in **although**.

altogether☆ *adverb*

> Watch out! An easy way to remember this is to break it into parts, **al-to-get-her.**

always *adverb*

amaze *verb* amazes, amazing, amazed

amazement *noun*

ambitious *adjective*

among *preposition*

amount *noun* amounts

amount *verb* amounts, amounting, amounted

amplification *noun*

amplifier *noun* amplifiers

amuse *verb* amuses, amusing, amused

an *determiner*

> You use **an** instead of **a** before a word beginning with a vowel sound, e.g. *an apple*, or before an abbreviation that sounds as though it begins with a vowel, e.g. *an MP.*

analyse *verb* analyses, analysing, analysed

ancestor *noun* ancestors

anchor *noun* anchors

ancient *adjective*

and *conjunction*

angel *noun* angels

anger *noun*

angle *noun* angles

angle *verb* angles, angling, angled

angrily *adverb*

angry *adjective* angrier, angriest

animal *noun* animals

ankle *noun* ankles

annoy *verb* annoys, annoying, annoyed

another *determiner, pronoun*

answer *noun* answers

answer *verb* answers, answering, answered

> Watch out! There is a silent **w** in **answer**. To make the past tense add **-ed** to **answer** = **answered**.

ant *noun* ants

antenna *noun*

> Watch out! The plural of **antenna** is **antennae**.

antique *noun* antiques

anxious *adjective*

any *determiner, pronoun, adverb*

anybody *pronoun*

anyhow *adverb*

anyone *pronoun*

anything *pronoun*

anyway *adverb*

anywhere *adverb*

apart *adverb*

apparent *adjective*

apparently *adverb*

appear *verb* appears, appearing, appeared

> Watch Out! There is a double **p** in **appear**.

appearance *noun* appearances

★ **Allowed** means to be permitted to do something. **Aloud** means in a voice that can be heard. *He read the letter aloud. Running in the corridors is not allowed.*

✪ An **altar** is a raised surface in religious ceremonies. **Alter** means to change something.

☆ **Altogether** is different from **all together**, which means together in a group *They wanted to be all together for the photographs.*

apple *noun* apples

applicable *adjective*

application *noun* applications

applied *adjective*

appreciate *verb* appreciates, appreciating, appreciated

approach *verb* approaches, approaching, approached

approach *noun* approaches

approve *verb* approves, approving, approved

arch *noun* arches

arch *verb* arches, arching, arched

are★

area *noun* areas

aren't

> Watch out! **Aren't = are + not.** Add an **apostrophe** between the **n** and **t**.

argue *verb* argues, arguing, argued

argument *noun* arguments

arm *noun* arms

arm *verb* arms, arming, armed

army *noun* armies

around *adverb, preposition*

arrange *verb* arranges, arranging, arranged

arrest *verb* arrests, arresting, arrested

arrest *noun* arrests

arrival *noun* arrivals

arrive *verb* arrives, arriving, arrived

> Watch Out! There is a double **r** in **arrive**.

arrow *noun* arrows

art *noun* arts

article *noun* articles

artificial *adjective*

artist *noun* artists

as *conjunction, adverb, preposition*

ascent✿ *noun* ascents

ash *noun* ashes

ashamed *adjective*

ashore *adverb*

aside *noun* asides

ask *verb* asks, asking, asked

asleep *adverb, adjective*

assent *noun*

assistance *noun*

assistant *noun* assistants

assume *verb* assumes, assuming, assumed

assumption *noun* assumptions

assure *verb* assures, assuring, assured

astonish *verb* astonishes, astonishing, astonished

astonishment *noun*

astronaut *noun* astronauts

at *preposition*

atmosphere *noun* atmospheres

attach *verb* attaches, attaching, attached

attack *noun* attacks

attack *verb* attacks, attacking, attacked

attempt *verb* attempts, attempting, attempted

attempt *noun* attempts

attend *verb* attends, attending, attended

attention *noun*

attic *noun* attics

attitude *noun* attitudes

attract *verb* attracts, attracting, attracted

audience *noun* audiences

aunt *noun* aunts

author *noun* authors

authority *noun* authorities

automobile *noun* automobiles

available *adjective*

average *noun* averages

avoid *verb* avoids, avoiding, avoided

avoidance *noun*

await *verb* awaits, awaiting, awaited

awake *verb* awakes, awaking, awoke, awoken

award *noun* awards

award *verb* awards, awarding, awarded

aware *adjective*

away *adverb, adjective*

awful *adjective*

★ Do not confuse **are** and **our**. *There are three cats. Our three cats are all tabbies.*
✿ An **ascent** is a climb up something and **assent** is agreement to something.

A
B
C
D
E
F
G
H
I
J
K
L
M
N
O
P
Q
R
S
T
U
V
W
X
Y
Z

awhile★ *adverb*

awkward *adjective*

Bb

baby *noun* babies

back *noun* backs

back *verb* backs, backing, backed

backwards *adverb*

badge *noun* badges

badly *adverb*

bag *noun* bags

bag *verb* bags, bagging, bagged

bake *verb* bakes, baking, baked

balance *noun* balances

balance *verb* balances, balancing, balanced

bale *noun* bales

bale☆ *verb* bales, baling, baled

ball *noun* balls

balloon *noun* balloons

> Double up! There is double **l** and double **o** in **balloon**.

band *noun* bands

band *verb* bands, banding, banded

bang *noun* bangs

bang *verb* bangs, banging, banged

bank *noun* banks

bank *verb* banks, banking, banked

bar *noun* bars

bar *verb* bars, barring, barred

bare✪ *adjective* barer, barest

barely *adverb*

bargain *noun* bargains

bargain *verb* bargains, bargaining, bargained

bark *noun* barks

bark *verb* barks, barking, barked

barn *noun* barns

barrel *noun* barrels

base *noun* bases

base☆ *verb* bases, basing, based

basic *adjective*

basically *adverb*

basket *noun* baskets

bass☆ *noun* basses

bat *noun* bats

bat *verb* bats, batting, batted

bath *noun* baths

bath *verb* baths, bathing, bathed

bathe *verb* bathes, bathing, bathed

> Watch out! **Bathe** sounds like **b-ay-the**.

bathe *noun* bathes

battery *noun* batteries

battle *noun* battles

bawl *verb* bawls, bawling, bawled

bay *noun* bays

beach* *noun* beaches

beak *noun* beaks

beam *noun* beams

beam *verb* beams, beaming, beamed

bean* *noun* beans

bear *verb* bears, bearing, bore, born or borne

bear✦ *noun* bears

beard *noun* beards

beast *noun* beasts

beat *verb* beats, beating, beat, beaten

beat *noun* beats

beautiful *adjective*

> The 'yoo' sound is spelt with the letter group **eau**. There is only one **l** too.

beauty *noun* beauties

because *conjunction*

> Tip! To spell **because** try: **b**ig **e**lephants **c**an **a**lways **u**nderstand **s**mall **e**lephants.

beckon *verb* beckons, beckoning, beckoned

become *verb* becomes, becoming, became, become

---

* ★ **Awhile** means for a short time, e.g. *Wait here awhile*. You use it as two words in e.g. *a short while*.
* ☆ **Bale** (noun) means a large bundle. **Bale** (verb) means to jump out of an aircraft.
* ✪ **Bare** means naked or not covered. A **bear** is an animal.
* ☆ **Base** means a place where things are controlled. **Bass** means a singer with a low voice.
* ✳ **Beach** means sandy part of the seashore. **Beech** is a type of a tree.
* ✱ A **bean** is a vegetable.
* ✦ To **bear** something is to carry it and a **bear** is an animal.

bed *noun* beds

bedroom *noun* bedrooms

bee *noun* bees

beetle *noun* beetles

before *adverb, preposition*

> Watch Out! **Before** ends with an **e**.

beg *verb* begs, begging, begged

begin *verb* begins, beginning, began, begun

beginner *noun* beginners

beginning *noun* beginnings

behave *verb* behaves, behaving, behaved

behind *noun* behinds

being *noun* beings

believe *verb* believes, believing, believed

> Tip! Think of this rule:
> i before e except after c
> when the sound is 'ee'.

bell *noun* bells

bellow *verb* bellows, bellowing, bellowed

belly *noun* bellies

belong *verb* belongs, belonging, belonged

below *preposition, adverb*

belt *noun* belts

belt *verb* belts, belting, belted

bench *noun* benches

bend *verb* bends, bending, bent

bend *noun* bends

beneath *preposition, adverb*

benefit *noun* benefits

benefit *verb* benefits, benefiting, benefited

berry *noun* berries

beside *preposition*

besides *preposition, adverb*

bet *noun* bets

bet *verb* bets, betting, bet or betted

betray *verb* betrays, betraying, betrayed

between *preposition, adverb*

beware *verb* beware

> **Beware** has no other forms.

beyond *preposition, adverb*

bicycle *noun* bicycles

bid *noun* bids

bid *verb* bids, bidding, bid

big *adjective* bigger, biggest

bike *noun* bikes

bill *noun* bills

bird *noun* birds

birth *noun* births

birthday *noun* birthdays

biscuit *noun* biscuits

bit *noun* bits

bite *verb* bites, biting, bit, bitten

bite★ *noun* bites

bitter *adjective*

black *adjective* blacker, blackest

black *noun* blacks

blackberry *noun* blackberries

blade *noun* blades

blame *verb* blames, blaming, blamed

blank *noun* blanks

blanket *noun* blankets

blast *noun* blasts

blast *verb* blasts, blasting, blasted

blaze *noun* blazes

blaze *verb* blazes, blazing, blazed

bleed *verb* bleeds, bleeding, bled

blemish *noun* blemishes

bless *verb* blesses, blessing, blessed

blind *adjective* blinder, blindest

blind *verb* blinds, blinding, blinded

blind *noun* blinds

blink *verb* blinks, blinking, blinked

block *noun* blocks

block *verb* blocks, blocking, blocked

blood *noun*

bloom *verb* blooms, blooming, bloomed

bloom *noun* blooms

blossom *noun* blossoms

blossom *verb* blossoms, blossoming, blossomed

blow *noun* blows

blow *verb* blows, blowing, blew, blown

> Watch out! The past tense of **blow** is **blew**. **Blue** is the colour.

blue *adjective* bluer, bluest

★ A **bite** is an act of biting. A **byte** is a unit in computing.

97

A B C D E F G H I J K L M N O P Q R S T U V W X Y Z

blue *noun* blues

> **Blue** is the colour. You use **blew** in, e.g. *the wind blew hard*. **Blew** is the past tense of **blow**.

board★ *noun* boards

board *verb* boards, boarding, boarded

body *noun* bodies

boil *verb* boils, boiling, boiled

boil *noun* boils

bold *adjective* bolder, boldest

bolt *noun* bolts

bolt *verb* bolts, bolting, bolted

bomb *noun* bombs

bomb *verb* bombs, bombing, bombed

bone *noun* bones

book *noun* books

book *verb* books, booking, booked

boom *noun* booms

boom *verb* booms, booming, boomed

boot *noun* boots

boot *verb* boots, booting, booted

border *noun* borders

borough *noun* boroughs

borrow *verb* borrows, borrowing, borrowed

both *determiner, pronoun, adverb*

bother *verb* bothers, bothering, bothered

bottle *noun* bottles

bottle *verb* bottles, bottling, bottled

bottom *noun* bottoms

bough✪ *noun* boughs

boulder *noun* boulders

> Watch Out! The long vowel sound 'oa' is spelt **ou** in **boulder**.

bounce *verb* bounces, bouncing, bounced

bounce *noun* bounces

boundary *noun* boundaries

bow✪ *noun* bows

bow *verb* bows, bowing, bowed

bowl *noun* bowls

bowl *verb* bowls, bowling, bowled

box *noun* boxes

box *verb* boxes, boxing, boxed

boy *noun* boys

brain *noun* brains

brake☆ *noun* brakes

branch *noun* branches

branch *verb* branches, branching, branched

brass *noun*

brave *adjective* braver, bravest

brave *noun* braves

breach✤ *noun* breaches

bread *noun*

break *verb* breaks, breaking, broke, broken

break☆ *noun* breaks

breakfast *noun* breakfasts

breast *noun* breasts

breath✦ *noun* breaths

breathe *verb* breathes, breathing, breathed

> Watch out! **Breathe** is pronounced br**ee**the.

breed *verb* breeds, breeding, bred

breed *noun* breeds

breeze *noun* breezes

brick *noun* bricks

bridal✻ *adjective*

bride *noun* brides

bridge *noun* bridges

bridle *noun* bridles

brief *adjective* briefer, briefest

brief *noun* briefs

brief *verb* briefs, briefing, briefed

bright *adjective* brighter, brightest

brilliant *adjective*

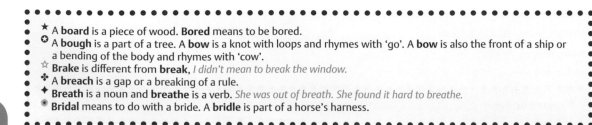

★ A **board** is a piece of wood. **Bored** means to be bored.
✪ A **bough** is a part of a tree. A **bow** is a knot with loops and rhymes with 'go'. A **bow** is also the front of a ship or a bending of the body and rhymes with 'cow'.
☆ **Brake** is different from **break**, *I didn't mean to break the window.*
✤ A **breach** is a gap or a breaking of a rule.
✦ **Breath** is a noun and **breathe** is a verb. *She was out of breath. She found it hard to breathe.*
✻ **Bridal** means to do with a bride. A **bridle** is part of a horse's harness.

bring *verb* brings, bringing, brought

broad *adjective* broader, broadest

brochure *noun* brochures

bronze *noun*

brook *noun* brooks

brother *noun* brothers

brow *noun* brows

brown *adjective* browner, brownest

bruise *noun* bruises

bruise *verb* bruises, bruising, bruised

brush *noun* brushes

brush *verb* brushes, brushing, brushed

bubble *noun* bubbles

bubble *verb* bubbles, bubbling, bubbled

bucket *noun* buckets

bug *noun* bugs

bug *verb* bugs, bugging, bugged

build *verb* builds, building, built

building *noun* buildings

bulb *noun* bulbs

bulge *noun* bulges

bulge *verb* bulges, bulging, bulged

bull *noun* bulls

bullet *noun* bullets

bully *verb* bullies, bullying, bullied

> **Watch Out!** When you add **-ing** to **bully** you keep the **-y**, **bullying**.

bully *noun* bullies

bun *noun* buns

bunch *noun* bunches

bunny *noun* bunnies

bureau *noun* bureaux

> Bureau is a French word used in English. It means a writing desk or an office.

burglar *noun* burglars

burn *verb* burns, burning, burnt or burned

burn *noun* burns

burrow *noun* burrows

burrow *verb* burrows, burrowing, burrowed

burst *verb* bursts, bursting, burst

> **Watch Out!** The past tense of **burst** is **burst**. Don't add **-ed**.

burst *noun* bursts

bury *verb* buries, burying, buried

bus *noun* buses

bush *noun* bushes

business *noun* businesses

but★ *conjunction, preposition*

butt★ *noun* butts

butt★ *verb* butts, butting, butted

butter *noun*

butterfly *noun* butterflies

> **Watch Out!** Don't add an apostrophe to make **butterflies**.

button *noun* buttons

button *verb* buttons, buttoning, buttoned

buy *verb* buys, buying, bought

> **Watch out!** The past tense of **buy** is **bought**.

buy *noun* buys

buzz *noun* buzzes

buzz *verb* buzzes, buzzing, buzzed

by *preposition, adverb*

bye✪ *noun* byes

Cc

cab *noun* cabs

cabin *noun* cabins

cactus *noun* cacti

> **Watch out!** The plural of **cactus** is **cacti**.

cage *noun* cages

calendar *noun* calendars

> **Watch the ending! Calendar** ends in **-ar**.

call *noun* calls

call *verb* calls, calling, called

★ You use **but** in, e.g. *I like fish but I'm not hungry.* A **butt** is part of a gun. **Butt** means to hit with your head.
✪ You use **by** in, e.g. *a book by J. K. Rowling.* You use **bye** in e.g. *bye for now.*

calm *adjective* calmer, calmest

Watch out! There is a silent **l** in **calm**.

camel *noun* camels

camera *noun* cameras

camp *noun* camps

camp *verb* camps, camping, camped

can *verb* cans, canning, canned

can *noun* cans

can't

Tip! **Can't** = **can** + **not**. Add an **apostrophe** between the **n** and **t**.

candle *noun* candles

candy *noun* candies

cannon *noun* cannon or cannons

canoe *noun* canoes

canoe *verb* canoes, canoeing, canoed

cap *noun* caps

cap *verb* caps, capping, capped

capital *noun* capitals

captain *noun* captains

capture *verb* captures, capturing, captured

car *noun* cars

carbon *noun*

card *noun* cards

care *noun* cares

care *verb* cares, caring, cared

career *noun* careers

career *verb* careers, careering, careered

careful *adjective*

carefully *adverb*

carpet *noun* carpets

carriage *noun* carriages

carry *verb* carries, carrying, carried

carve★ *verb* carves, carving, carved

case *noun* cases

cast *verb* casts, casting, cast

cast *noun* casts

castle *noun* castles

catch *verb* catches, catching, caught

Watch out! The past tense of catch is **caught** and the 'or' sound is spelt **augh**.

catch *noun* catches

cattle *plural noun*

cause *noun* causes

cause *verb* causes, causing, caused

cautious *adjective*

cautiously *adverb*

cave *noun* caves

cave *verb* caves, caving, caved

cavern *noun* caverns

cease *verb* ceases, ceasing, ceased

ceiling *noun* ceilings

Follow the rule: **i before e except after c** in **ceiling**.

celebrate *verb* celebrates, celebrating, celebrated

cell✪ *noun* cells

cellar☆ *noun* cellars

central *adjective*

centre *noun* centres

centre *verb* centres, centring, centred

century *noun* centuries

cereal✤ *noun* cereals

ceremony *noun* ceremonies

certain *adjective*

Watch out! **Certain** ends in **-ain**.

certainly *adverb*

chain *noun* chains

chair *noun* chairs

chalet *noun* chalets

chalky *adjective*

challenge *verb* challenges, challenging, challenged

challenge *noun* challenges

chamber *noun* chambers

chance *noun* chances

change *verb* changes, changing, changed

change *noun* changes

changeable *adjective*

chant *noun* chants

★ You use **carves** in, e.g. *He carves the meat with a knife.* **Calves** are a part of your leg.
✪ A **cell** is a small room or part of an organism. To **sell** something means to exchange it for money.
☆ A **cellar** is a room under a house. A **seller** is someone who sells something.
✤ A **cereal** is something you eat. A **serial** is a story or programme in separate parts.

chant *verb* chants, chanting, chanted

chap *noun* chaps

chapter *noun* chapters

character *noun* characters

charge *noun* charges

charge *verb* charges, charging, charged

chariot *noun* chariots

charm *noun* charms

charm *verb* charms, charming, charmed

chase *verb* chases, chasing, chased

chase *noun* chases

chat *noun* chats

chat *verb* chats, chatting, chatted

chatter *verb* chatters, chattering, chattered

chauffeur *noun* chauffeurs

cheap *adjective* cheaper, cheapest

check *verb* checks, checking, checked

check *noun* checks

cheek *noun* cheeks

cheek *verb* cheeks, cheeking, cheeked

cheer *noun* cheers

cheer *verb* cheers, cheering, cheered

cheerful *adjective*

cheese *noun* cheeses

chef *noun* chefs

chemical *noun* chemicals

chemist *noun* chemists

chest *noun* chests

chew *verb* chews, chewing, chewed

chicken *noun* chickens

chicken *verb* chickens, chickening, chickened

chief *noun* chiefs

child *noun* children

chill *noun* chills

chill *verb* chills, chilling, chilled

chimney *noun* chimneys

> Watch out! The plural of **chimney** is **chimneys**.

chin *noun* chins

chip *noun* chips

chip *verb* chips, chipping, chipped

chocolate *noun* chocolates

> Tip! There is an **o** in **chocolate: choc-o-late**.

choice *noun* choices

choke *verb* chokes, choking, choked

choke *noun* chokes

choose *verb* chooses, choosing, chose, chosen

chord★ *noun* chords

> The 'k' sound is spelt **ch-** in **chord**.

chorus *noun* choruses

Christmas *noun* Christmases

chuckle *verb* chuckles, chuckling, chuckled

chuckle *noun* chuckles

church *noun* churches

circle *noun* circles

circle *verb* circles, circling, circled

circuit *noun* circuits

circumstance *noun* circumstances

circus *noun* circuses

city *noun* cities

> Watch out! The plural of **city** is **cities**.

civilization *noun* civilizations

claim *verb* claims, claiming, claimed

claim *noun* claims

clap *verb* claps, clapping, clapped

clap *noun* claps

clasp *verb* clasps, clasping, clasped

clasp *noun* clasps

class *noun* classes

class *verb* classes, classing, classed

clatter *verb* clatters, clattering, clattered

claw✿ *noun* claws

claw✿ *verb* claws, clawing, clawed

clay *noun*

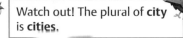

★ A **cord** is a piece of thin rope. A **chord** is a number of musical notes played together.

✿ **Claws** (noun) are the hard sharp nails that some animals have on their feet. To **claw** (verb) is to scratch, maul, or pull a person or thing. A **clause** is part of a sentence or contract.

A B C D E F G H I J K L M N O P Q R S T U V W X Y Z

clean *adjective* cleaner, cleanest

clean *verb* cleans, cleaning, cleaned

cleanser *noun*

clear *adjective* clearer, clearest

clear *verb* clears, clearing, cleared

clearly *adverb*

clench *verb* clenches, clenching, clenched

clever *adjective* cleverer, cleverest

click *noun* clicks

click *verb* clicks, clicking, clicked

cliff *noun* cliffs

climate *noun* climates

climb *verb* climbs, climbing, climbed

> Watch out! There is a silent **b** in **climb**.

climb *noun* climbs

cling *verb* clings, clinging, clung

cloak *noun* cloaks

clock *noun* clocks

close *adjective* closer, closest

close *verb* closes, closing, closed

closely *adverb*

cloth *noun* cloths

clothes *plural noun*

> Watch out! **Clothes** is plural and ends in **-es**.

clothing *noun*

cloud *noun* clouds

cloud *verb* clouds, clouding, clouded

club *noun* clubs

club *verb* clubs, clubbing, clubbed

clue *noun* clues

clutch *verb* clutches, clutching, clutched

clutch *noun* clutches

coach *noun* coaches

coach *verb* coaches, coaching, coached

coal *noun*

coast *noun* coasts

coast *verb* coasts, coasting, coasted

coat *noun* coats

coat *verb* coats, coating, coated

code *noun* codes

code *verb* codes, coding, coded

coffee *noun* coffees

coil *noun* coils

coil *verb* coils, coiling, coiled

coin *noun* coins

coin *verb* coins, coining, coined

cold *adjective* colder, coldest

cold *noun* colds

collapse *verb* collapses, collapsing, collapsed

collapse *noun* collapses

collar *noun* collars

collect *verb* collects, collecting, collected

collection *noun* collections

college *noun* colleges

collision *noun* collisions

colonel★ *noun* colonels

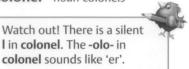

> Watch out! There is a silent **l** in **colonel**. The **-olo-** in **colonel** sounds like 'er'.

colony *noun* colonies

colour *noun* colours

> Watch out! The 'ur' sound is spelt **-our** in **colour**.

colour *verb* colours, colouring, coloured

column *noun* columns

> Watch out! There is a silent **n** in **column**.

comb *noun* combs

comb *verb* combs, combing, combed

come *verb* comes, coming, came, come

> Watch Out! The 'u' sound is spelt with an **o** in **come**, **coming**.

comfort *verb* comforts, comforting, comforted

comfortable *adjective*

comically *adverb*

command *noun* commands

command *verb* commands, commanding, commanded

comment *noun* comments

★ A **colonel** is an army officer. **Kernel** is part of a nut.

committee *noun* committees

> Double it! Double **m**, double **t** and double **e** in **committee**.

common *adjective* commoner, commonest

common *noun* commons

companion *noun* companions

company *noun* companies

compare *verb* compares, comparing, compared

competition *noun* competitions

> Watch Out! The 'shun' sound is spelt **-tion** in **competition**.

complain *verb* complains, complaining, complained

complement☉ *noun* complements

complete *verb* completes, completing, completed

> Watch out! The 'ee' sound is spelt **ete** in **complete**.

completely *adverb*

> Tip! Start with **complete** and add **-ly** to spell **completely**.

completion *noun*

compliment☉ *noun* compliments

comprehension *noun* comprehensions

computer *noun* computers

comrade *noun* comrades

conceal *verb* conceals, concealing, concealed

conceive *verb* conceives, conceiving, conceived

concentrate *verb* concentrates, concentrating, concentrated

concern *verb* concerns, concerning, concerned

concern *noun* concerns

concrete *noun, adjective*

condition *noun* conditions

confess *verb* confesses, confessing, confessed

confession *noun* confessions

confidence *noun*

confident *adjective*

confidential *adjective*

confuse *verb* confuses, confusing, confused

confusion *noun*

congratulate *verb* congratulates, congratulating, congratulated

conker☉ *noun* conkers

connect *verb* connects, connecting, connected

conquer☉ *verb* conquers, conquering, conquered

conscience *noun*

conscious *adjective*

consciousness *noun*

> Watch out! **Conscious** has **sci** in the middle.

consent *verb* consents, consenting, consented

consider *verb* considers, considering, considered

considerable *adjective*

consideration *noun* considerations

constancy *noun*

contact *noun* contacts

contact *verb* contacts, contacting, contacted

contain *verb* contains, containing, contained

content *noun, adjective*

continent *noun* continents

continue *verb* continues, continuing, continued

control *noun* controls

control *verb* controls, controlling, controlled

conversation *noun* conversations

convince *verb* convinces, convincing, convinced

cook *verb* cooks, cooking, cooked

cook *noun* cooks

cool *adjective* cooler, coolest

cool *verb* cools, cooling, cooled

copier *noun*

copper *noun* coppers

copy *noun* copies

copy *verb* copies, copying, copied

corn *noun* corns

corner *noun* corners

corner *verb* corners, cornering, cornered

a b **c** d e f g h i j k l m n o p q r s t u v w x y z

★ A **complement** is a thing that completes something. A **compliment** is something good you say about someone.
☉ A **conker** is the fruit of a horse chestnut tree. To **conquer** means to invade or take over.

A
B
C
D
E
F
G
H
I
J
K
L
M
N
O
P
Q
R
S
T
U
V
W
X
Y
Z

correct *verb* corrects, correcting, corrected

correction *noun* corrections

correspond *verb* corresponds, corresponding, corresponded

corridor *noun* corridors

cost *verb* costs, costing, cost

cost *noun* costs

costume *noun* costumes

cosy *adjective* cosier, cosiest

cosy *noun* cosies

cottage *noun* cottages

cotton *noun*

cough *verb* coughs, coughing, coughed

cough *noun* coughs

Watch out! The ending is spelt **-ough** in **cough**.

could *verb*

couldn't

Tip! **Couldn't = could + not.** Add an **apostrophe** between the **n** and **t**.

count *verb* counts, counting, counted

count *noun* counts

counter *noun* counters

country *noun* countries

couple *noun* couples

couple *verb* couples, coupling, coupled

courage *noun*

courageous *adjective*

court *noun* courts

court *verb* courts, courting, courted

courtyard *noun* courtyards

cousin *noun* cousins

cover *verb* covers, covering, covered

Tip! Start with **cover** and add **-ed** to spell **covered**.

cover *noun* covers

cow *noun* cows

crab *noun* crabs

crack *noun* cracks

crack *verb* cracks, cracking, cracked

craft *noun* crafts

crash *noun* crashes

crash *verb* crashes, crashing, crashed

crawl *verb* crawls, crawling, crawled

crazy *adjective* crazier, craziest

creak *noun* creaks

creak *verb* creaks, creaking, creaked

creaky *adjective*

cream *noun* creams

create *verb* creates, creating, created

creativity *noun*

creature *noun* creatures

creep *verb* creeps, creeping, crept

Watch out! The past tense of **creep** is **crept**.

creep *noun* creeps

crew *noun* crews

crime *noun* crimes

criss-cross *adjective, adverb*

critic *noun* critics

crocodile *noun* crocodiles

crop *noun* crops

crop *verb* crops, cropping, cropped

cross *noun* crosses

cross *verb* crosses, crossing, crossed

crouch *verb* crouches, crouching, crouched

crow *noun* crows

crow *verb* crows, crowing, crowed

crowd *noun* crowds

crowd *verb* crowds, crowding, crowded

crown *noun* crowns

crown *verb* crowns, crowning, crowned

cruel *adjective* crueller, cruellest

crunch *noun* crunches

crunch *verb* crunches, crunching, crunched

crunchy *adjective*

crush *verb* crushes, crushing, crushed

crush *noun* crushes

cry *verb* cries, crying, cried

Watch out! The past tense of **cry** is **cried**.

cry *noun* cries

crystal *noun* crystals

cube *noun* cubes

cube *verb* cubes, cubing, cubed

cup *noun* cups

cup *verb* cups, cupping, cupped

cupboard *noun* cupboards

cure *verb* cures, curing, cured

cure *noun* cures

curiosity *noun* curiosities

curious *adjective*

curiously *adverb*

curl *noun* curls

curl *verb* curls, curling, curled

currant★ *noun* currants

current *noun* currents

curse *noun* curses

curse *verb* curses, cursing, cursed

curtain *noun* curtains

curve *noun* curves

curve *verb* curves, curving, curved

cushion *noun* cushions

cushion *verb* cushions, cushioning, cushioned

custom *noun* customs

cut *verb* cuts, cutting, cut

cut *noun* cuts

cute *adjective* cuter, cutest

Dd

damage *verb* damages, damaging, damaged

damp *adjective* damper, dampest

dance *verb* dances, dancing, danced

dance *noun* dances

danger *noun* dangers

dangerous *adjective*

dangle *verb* dangles, dangling, dangled

dare *verb* dares, daring, dared

dare *noun* dares

dark *adjective* darker, darkest

darkness *noun*

darling *noun* darlings

dart *noun* darts

dash *noun* dashes

dash *verb* dashes, dashing, dashed

date *noun* dates

date *verb* dates, dating, dated

daughter *noun* daughters

dawn *noun* dawns

dawn *verb* dawns, dawning, dawned

day *noun* days

daylight *noun*

dead *adjective*

deadly *adjective* deadlier, deadliest

deafness *noun*

deal *verb* deals, dealing, dealt

deal *noun* deals

dear✪ *adjective* dearer, dearest

death *noun* deaths

debate *noun* debates

debate *verb* debates, debating, debated

deceive *verb* deceives, deceiving, deceived

> Follow the rule: **i before e except after c** in **deceive**.

decency *noun*

decent *adjective*

decide *verb* decides, deciding, decided

> Watch out! The 's' sound is spelt with **c** in **decide**. To make the past tense, start with **decide**, take off the **-e** and add **-ed**, **decided**.

decimal *noun* decimals

decision *noun* decisions

deck *noun* decks

declare *verb* declares, declaring, declared

decorate *verb* decorates, decorating, decorated

deed *noun* deeds

deep *adjective* deeper, deepest

deeply *adverb*

deer✪ *noun* deer

defeat *verb* defeats, defeating, defeated

defeat *noun* defeats

defend *verb* defends, defending, defended

definite *adjective*

definitely *adverb, interjection*

> Watch out! **Definite** ends in **-ite**, then add **-ly**, **definitely**.

a b **c** d e f g h i j k l m n o p q r s t u v w x y z

★ A **currant** is a small dried grape. A **current** is a flow of water, air or electricity. Something that is **current** is happening now.

✪ **Dear** means loved or expensive. A **deer** is an animal.

A B C D E F G H I J K L M N O P Q R S T U V W X Y Z

degree *noun* degrees

delay *verb* delays, delaying, delayed

delay *noun* delays

delicate *adjective*

delicious *adjective*

delight *verb* delights, delighting, delighted

delight *noun* delights

delightful *adjective*

deliver *verb* delivers, delivering, delivered

demand *verb* demands, demanding, demanded

demand *noun* demands

demon *noun* demons

demonstrate *verb* demonstrates, demonstrating, demonstrated

den *noun* dens

dense *adjective* denser, densest

deny *verb* denies, denying, denied

departure *noun*

depend *verb* depends, depending, depended

dependable *adjective*

dependant *noun* dependants

dependence *noun*

dependent★ *adjective*

deprive *verb* deprives, depriving, deprived

depth *noun* depths

descend *verb* descends, descending, descended

descent✪ *noun* descents

describe *verb* describes, describing, described

> Watch out! This word is spelt **de** + **scribe**.

desert *noun* deserts

desert☆ *verb* deserts, deserting, deserted

deserve *verb* deserves, deserving, deserved

design *noun* designs

design *verb* designs, designing, designed

> Watch out! There is a silent **g** in **design**.

desk *noun* desks

despair *verb* despairs, despairing, despaired

desperate *adjective*

> Watch out! There is an **e** in the middle of **desp-e-rate**.

desperately *adverb*

despite *preposition*

dessert☆ *noun* desserts

destroy *verb* destroys, destroying, destroyed

destruction *noun*

detail *noun* details

determine *verb* determines, determining, determined

develop *verb* develops, developing, developed

> Watch out! There is no **e** at the end of **develop**.

device *noun* devices

devil *noun* devils

devise *verb* devises, devising, devised

diamond *noun* diamonds

> Watch Out! There is an **a** in **diamond**.

dictionary *noun* dictionaries

didn't

> Tip! **Didn't** = **did** + **not**. Add an **apostrophe** between the **n** and **t**.

die✱ *verb* dies, dying, died

> Watch out! Change the **-ie** to **-y** and add **-ing** for **dying**.

diesel *noun* diesels

difference *noun* differences

different *adjective*

> Watch Out! There is an **-er** in the middle of **diff-er-ent**.

difficult *adjective*

difficulty *noun* difficulties

dig *verb* digs, digging, dug

dig *noun* digs

★ **Dependant** is a noun: *She has three dependants.* **Dependent** is an adjective: *She has three dependent children.*

✪ A **descent** is a climb down. **Dissent** is to disagree.

☆ A **dessert** is a sweet pudding. To **desert** [verb] is to abandon or leave without asking. A **desert** [noun] is a very dry area of land.

✱ **Die** means to stop living. **Dye** means to change the colour of something.

dim *adjective* dimmer, dimmest

dim *verb* dims, dimming, dimmed

dine *verb* dines, dining, dined

diner ★ *noun*

dinner ★ *noun* dinners

dinosaur *noun* dinosaurs

dip *verb* dips, dipping, dipped

dip *noun* dips

direct *verb* directs, directing, directed

direction *noun* directions

directly *adverb*

dirt *noun*

dirty *adjective* dirtier, dirtiest

disappear *verb* disappears, disappearing, disappeared

> Double up the p! **Disappear** = dis + appear.

disappoint *verb* disappoints, disappointing, disappointed

> Double up the p! **Disappoint** = dis + appoint.

disappointment *noun*

disarm *verb* disarms, disarming, disarmed

disarmament *noun*

disaster *noun* disasters

disciple *noun* disciples

discover *verb* discovers, discovering, discovered

discovery *noun* discoveries

discuss *verb* discusses, discussing, discussed

discussion *noun* discussions

disease *noun* diseases

disguise *verb* disguises, disguising, disguised

disguise *noun* disguises

disgust *verb* disgusts, disgusting, disgusted

dish *noun* dishes

dish *verb* dishes, dishing, dished

disinterested ✿ *adjective*

disobey *verb* disobeys, disobeying, disobeyed

display *verb* displays, displaying, displayed

display *noun* displays

dissent ☆ *verb, noun*

distance *noun* distances

distant *adjective*

distract *verb* distracts, distracting, distracted

distress *verb* distresses, distressing, distressed

disturb *verb* disturbs, disturbing, disturbed

ditch *noun* ditches

dive *verb* dives, diving, dived

divide *verb* divides, dividing, divided

division *noun* divisions

do *verb* does, doing, did, done

> Watch Out! The past tense of **do** is **did**.

dock *verb* docks, docking, docked

doctor *noun* doctors

document *noun* documents

dodge *verb* dodges, dodging, dodged

dodge *noun* dodges

doe ✤ *noun* does

does *verb*

doesn't

> Tip! **Doesn't = does + not.** Add an **apostrophe** between the **n** and **t**.

dog *noun* dogs

doll *noun* dolls

dollar *noun* dollars

dolphin *noun* dolphins

dome *noun* domes

don't

> Tip! **Don't = do + not.** Add an **apostrophe** between the **n** and **t**.

donkey *noun* donkeys

door *noun* doors

doorway *noun* doorways

dot *noun* dots

dot *verb* dots, dotting, dotted

a
b
c
d
e
f
g
h
i
j
k
l
m
n
o
p
q
r
s
t
u
v
w
x
y
z

- ★ A **diner** is someone who eats dinner. **Dinner** is a meal.
- ✿ **Disinterested** means impartial and **uninterested** means not interested or bored.
- ☆ **Dissent** is to disagree. A **descent** is a climb down.
- ✤ A **doe** is a female deer. **Dough** is a mixture of flour and water used for baking.

A B C D E F G H I J K L M N O P Q R S T U V W X Y Z

double *noun* doubles

double *verb* doubles, doubling, doubled

doubt *noun* doubts

> Watch out! There is a silent **b** in **doubt**.

doubt *verb* doubts, doubting, doubted

down *adverb*, *preposition*, *noun*

downstairs *adverb*, *adjective*

dozen *noun* dozens

draft★ *noun* drafts

draft *verb* drafts, drafting, drafted

drag *verb* drags, dragging, dragged

dragon *noun* dragons

drain *noun* drains

drain *verb* drains, draining, drained

dramatically *adverb*

draught★ *noun* draughts

> Watch out! This word sounds like **draft**.

draw *verb* draws, drawing, drew, drawn

> Watch out! The past tense of **draw** is **drew**.

draw *noun* draws

drawer *noun* drawers

drawing *noun* drawings

dread *verb* dreads, dreading, dreaded

dreadful *adjective*

dream *noun* dreams

dream *verb* dreams, dreaming, dreamt or dreamed

dress *noun* dresses

dress *verb* dresses, dressing, dressed

drier *noun* driers

drift *verb* drifts, drifting, drifted

drift *noun* drifts

drink *verb* drinks, drinking, drank, drunk

drink *noun* drinks

drip *verb* drips, dripping, dripped

drip *noun* drips

drive *verb* drives, driving, drove, driven

> Watch out! The past tense of **drive** is **drove**.

drive *noun* drives

driver *noun*

drop *noun* drops

drop *verb* drops, dropping, dropped

> Watch Out! Double up the **p** when adding **-ing** or **-ed**.

drown *verb* drowns, drowning, drowned

drowsiness *noun*

drug *noun* drugs

drug *verb* drugs, drugging, drugged

drum *noun* drums

drum *verb* drums, drumming, drummed

dry *adjective* drier, driest

dry *verb* dries, drying, dried

dryness *noun*

duck *noun* ducks

duck *verb* ducks, ducking, ducked

due✪ *adjective*, *adverb*

dull *adjective* duller, dullest

dump *noun* dumps

dump *verb* dumps, dumping, dumped

during *preposition*

dust *verb* dusts, dusting, dusted

dusty *adjective* dustier, dustiest

duty *noun* duties

Ee

eager *adjective*

eagerly *adverb*

eagle *noun* eagles

ear *noun* ears

early *adverb*, *adjective* earlier, earliest

> Watch out! The 'ur' sound is spelt **-ear** in **early**.

earn *verb* earns, earning, earned

> Watch out! The 'ur' sound is spelt **-ear** in **earn**.

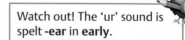

★ A **draft** is a first version of something. To **draft** something is to complete it in rough. A **draught** is a current of air.
✪ **Dew** is moisture on grass and plants. **Due** means expected.

earth *noun* earths

> Watch out! The 'ur' sound is spelt **-ear** in **earth**.

earthquake *noun* earthquakes

ease *verb* eases, easing, eased

easily *adverb*

east *noun, adjective, adverb*

easy *adjective* easier, easiest

> Watch out! Change the **-y** to **-i**, and add **-er** or **-est**, **easier**, **easiest**.

eat *verb* eats, eating, ate, eaten

> Watch out! The past tense of **eat** is **ate**.

echo *noun* echoes

echo *verb* echoes, echoing, echoed

ecstasy *noun* ecstasies

> Not many words end in **-asy**.

edge *noun* edges

edge *verb* edges, edging, edged

educate *verb* educates, educating, educated

education *noun*

effect★ *noun* effects

effort *noun* efforts

egg *noun* eggs

egg *verb* eggs, egging, egged

either *determiner, pronoun, adverb, conjunction*

elbow *noun* elbows

elbow *verb* elbows, elbowing, elbowed

electric *adjective*

electrically *adverb*

electrician *noun* electricians

electricity *noun*

electronically *adverb*

elephant *noun* elephants

eligible *adjective*

eliminate *verb* eliminates, eliminating, eliminated

elimination *noun*

else *adverb*

email *noun* emails

email *verb* emails, emailing, emailed

embarrass *verb* embarrasses, embarrassing, embarrassed

> Double up! There is double **r** and double **s** in **embarrass**.

emerge *verb* emerges, emerging, emerged

emigrate *verb* emigrates, emigrating, emigrated

emission *noun* emissions

emotion *noun* emotions

emperor *noun* emperors

empire *noun* empires

empty *adjective* emptier, emptiest

empty *verb* empties, emptying, emptied

enclosure *noun* enclosures

encounter *verb* encounters, encountering, encountered

encourage *verb* encourages, encouraging, encouraged

end *noun* ends

end *verb* ends, ending, ended

endure *verb* endures, enduring, endured

enemy *noun* enemies

energetically *adverb*

energy *noun* energies

engine *noun* engines

engineer *noun* engineers

enjoy *verb* enjoys, enjoying, enjoyed

enjoyable *adjective*

enjoyment *noun*

enormous *adjective*

enough *determiner, noun, adverb*

> Watch out! The ending is spelt **-ough** in **enough**.

enquire *verb* enquires, enquiring, enquired

enquiry✪ *noun* enquiries

enrol *verb* enrols, enrolling, enrolled

enter *verb* enters, entering, entered

entire *adjective*

entirely *adverb*

entirety *noun*

entrance *noun* entrances

a b c d e f g h i j k l m n o p q r s t u v w x y z

★ An **effect** (noun) is something that is caused by something else. **Affect** (verb) means to make something change.
✪ An **enquiry** is a question. An **inquiry** is an official investigation.

A B C D **E** F G H I J K L M N O P Q R S T U V W X Y Z

entrance *verb* entrances, entrancing, entranced

entry *noun* entries

envelope *noun* envelopes

envious *adjective*

environment *noun* environments

Watch out! There is an **n** in the middle of **environment**.

equal *noun* equals

equal *verb* equals, equalling, equalled

equator *noun*

equip *verb* equips, equipping, equipped

equipment *noun*

escape *verb* escapes, escaping, escaped

escape *noun* escapes

especially *adverb*

essential *noun* essentials

estimate *noun* estimates

estimate *verb* estimates, estimating, estimated

eternally *adverb*

evaporation *noun*

even *verb* evens, evening, evened

evening *noun* evenings

event *noun* events

eventually *adverb*

ever *adverb*

every *determiner*

Watch Out! **Every** has **er** in the middle, **ev-er-y**.

everybody *pronoun*

everyone *pronoun*

Watch Out! **Everyone** has **er** in the middle, **ev-er-y-one**.

everything *pronoun*

everywhere *adverb*

evidence *noun*

evidently *adverb*

evil *noun* evils

exactly *adverb*

exaggerate *verb* exaggerates, exaggerating, exaggerated

exaggeration *noun*

examine *verb* examines, examining, examined

example *noun* examples

excavate *verb* excavates, excavating, excavated

exceed *verb* exceeds, exceeding, exceeded

Watch out! The 's' sound is spelt with **c** in **ex-ceed**.

excellent *adjective*

except★ *preposition*

Watch out! The 's' sound is spelt with **c** in **ex-cept**.

exception *noun* exceptions

exchange *verb* exchanges, exchanging, exchanged

exchange *noun* exchanges

excite *verb* excites, exciting, excited

Watch out! The 's' sound is spelt with **c** in **ex-cite**.

excitement *noun* excitements

Watch out! The 's' sound is spelt with **c** and you keep the **e** in **excitement**.

exclaim *verb* exclaims, exclaiming, exclaimed

excuse *noun* excuses

excuse *verb* excuses, excusing, excused

exercise *noun* exercises

exercise *verb* exercises, exercising, exercised

exist *verb* exists, existing, existed

expansion *noun*

expect *verb* expects, expecting, expected

expectant *adjective*

expectation *noun* expectations

expensive *adjective*

experience *noun* experiences

experience *verb* experiences, experiencing, experienced

experiment *noun* experiments

experiment *verb* experiments, experimenting, experimented

explain *verb* explains, explaining, explained

explanation *noun* explanations

★ **Except** is different from **accept**: **except** means other than, *everyone except me*, to **accept** something is to take it.

explode *verb* explodes, exploding, exploded

explore *verb* explores, exploring, explored

explosion *noun* explosions

express *noun* expresses

express *verb* expresses, expressing, expressed

expression *noun* expressions

extend *verb* extends, extending, extended

extension *noun* extensions

extra *noun* extras

extraordinary *adjective*

extreme *noun* extremes

extremely *adverb*

> Watch Out! The long vowel **e** sound is spelt '**e-e**' in **extreme**.

eye *noun* eyes

eye *verb* eyes, eyeing, eyed

Ff

face *noun* faces

face *verb* faces, facing, faced

fact *noun* facts

factory *noun* factories

fade *verb* fades, fading, faded

fail *verb* fails, failing, failed

fail *noun* fails

faint *adjective* fainter, faintest

faint *verb* faints, fainting, fainted

fair *adjective* fairer, fairest

fair *noun* fairs

fairly *adverb*

fairy *noun* fairies

faith *noun* faiths

faithfulness *noun*

fall *verb* falls, falling, fell, fallen

> Watch out! The past tense of **fall** is **fell**.

fall *noun* falls

familiar *adjective*

family *noun* families

famous *adjective*

fan *noun* fans

fan *verb* fans, fanning, fanned

fancy *noun* fancies

fancy *adjective* fancier, fanciest

fancy *verb* fancies, fancying, fancied

fantastic *adjective*

fare *noun* fares

fare *verb* fares, faring, fared

farewell *interjection*

farm *noun* farms

farm *verb* farms, farming, farmed

farmer *noun* farmers

farmyard *noun* farmyards

farther *adverb, adjective*

> Watch out! It is easy to confuse **farther** and **father**. You can use **farther** or **further** in *farther up the road*. **Father** is a parent.

fascinate *verb* fascinates, fascinating, fascinated

> Watch out! There is **sci** in the middle of **fascinate**.

fashion *noun* fashions

fashion *verb* fashions, fashioning, fashioned

fast *adjective* faster, fastest

fast *verb* fasts, fasting, fasted

fasten *verb* fastens, fastening, fastened

fat *noun* fats

fat *adjective* fatter, fattest

fate★ *noun* fates

father *noun* fathers

father-in-law *noun* fathers-in-law

fault *noun* faults

fault *verb* faults, faulting, faulted

favour *noun* favours

favour *verb* favours, favouring, favoured

favourite *noun* favourites

> Watch Out! There are three syllables to spell in **favourite**: **fav-ou-rite**.

fear *noun* fears

fear *verb* fears, fearing, feared

feast *noun* feasts

feast *verb* feasts, feasting, feasted

feat✪ *noun* feats

feather *noun* feathers

a b c d e f g h i j k l m n o p q r s t u v w x y z

★ **Fate** is a power that is thought to make things happen. A **fete** is an outdoor entertainment with stalls.
✪ A **feat** is an achievement. **Feet** is the plural of foot.

A
B
C
D
E
F
G
H
I
J
K
L
M
N
O
P
Q
R
S
T
U
V
W
X
Y
Z

feature *noun* features

feature *verb* features, featuring, featured

feed *verb* feeds, feeding, fed

feed *noun* feeds

feel *verb* feels, feeling, felt

> Watch out! The past tense of **feel** is **felt**.

feeler *noun* feelers

fellow *noun* fellows

fence *noun* fences

fence *verb* fences, fencing, fenced

fern *noun* ferns

fertilization *noun*

festival *noun* festivals

fetch *verb* fetches, fetching, fetched

fete *noun* fetes

> **Fate** is a power that is thought to make things happen. A **fete** is an outdoor entertainment with stalls.

fever *noun* fevers

few *determiner* fewer, fewest

fiction *noun* fictions

fictional *adjective*

fictitious *adjective*

field *noun* fields

field *verb* fields, fielding, fielded

fieldwork *noun*

fiendish *adjective*

fiendishly *adverb*

fierce *adjective* fiercer, fiercest

fight *noun* fights

fight *verb* fights, fighting, fought

> Watch out! The past tense of **fight** is **fought**.

figure *noun* figures

figure *verb* figures, figuring, figured

file *noun* files

file *verb* files, filing, filed

fill *verb* fills, filling, filled

fill *noun* fills

film *noun* films

film *verb* films, filming, filmed

final *noun* finals

finally *adverb*

> Tip! Start with **final** and add **-ly** to make **finally**.

find *verb* finds, finding, found

findings *plural noun*

fine *adjective* finer, finest

fine *noun* fines

fine *verb* fines, fining, fined

finger *noun* fingers

finish *verb* finishes, finishing, finished

> Watch Out! There is an **i** on both sides of the **n**, in **finished**.

finish *noun* finishes

fire *noun* fires

fire *verb* fires, firing, fired

firm *noun* firms

firm *adjective* firmer, firmest

first *adjective, adverb, noun*

fish *noun* fish or fishes

fish *verb* fishes, fishing, fished

fist *noun* fists

fit *adjective* fitter, fittest

fit *verb* fits, fitting, fitted

fit *noun* fits

fix *verb* fixes, fixing, fixed

fix *noun* fixes

flag *noun* flags

flag *verb* flags, flagging, flagged

flame *noun* flames

flame *verb* flames, flaming, flamed

flap *noun* flaps

flap *verb* flaps, flapping, flapped

flash *noun* flashes

flash *verb* flashes, flashing, flashed

flat *adjective* flatter, flattest

flat *noun* flats

flavour *noun* flavours

flavour *verb* flavours, flavouring, flavoured

flee★ *verb* flees, fleeing, fled

flesh *noun*

flicker *verb* flickers, flickering, flickered

flight *noun* flights

fling *verb* flings, flinging, flung

float *verb* floats, floating, floated

float *noun* floats

flock *noun* flocks

★ To **flee** is to run away. A **flea** is an insect.

flock *verb* flocks, flocking, flocked

flood *noun* floods

flood *verb* floods, flooding, flooded

floor *noun* floors

floor *verb* floors, flooring, floored

flour★ *noun*

flow *verb* flows, flowing, flowed

flow *noun* flows

flower★ *noun* flowers

flower *verb* flowers, flowering, flowered

flu✪ *noun*

flue *noun* flues

flush *verb* flushes, flushing, flushed

flush *noun* flushes

flutter *verb* flutters, fluttering, fluttered

flutter *noun* flutters

fly *verb* flies, flying, flew, flown

fly *noun* flies

focus *noun* focuses or foci

focus *verb* focuses, focusing, focused

fodder *noun*

fog *noun* fogs

fold *verb* folds, folding, folded

fold *noun* folds

folk *plural noun*

follow *verb* follows, following, followed

fond *adjective* fonder, fondest

food *noun* foods

fool *noun* fools

fool *verb* fools, fooling, fooled

foolish *adjective*

foot *noun* feet

football *noun* footballs

footstep *noun* footsteps

for☆ *preposition, conjunction*

forbid *verb* forbids, forbidding, forbade, forbidden

forcible *adjective*

fore☆ *adjective, noun*

forehead *noun* foreheads

foreign *adjective*

forest *noun* forests

forever✤ *adverb*

forget *verb* forgets, forgetting, forgot, forgotten

forgive *verb* forgives, forgiving, forgave, forgiven

fork *noun* forks

fork *verb* forks, forking, forked

form *noun* forms

form *verb* forms, forming, formed

formality *noun*

format *noun* formats

former *adjective*

fort *noun* forts

forth *adverb*

fortieth *adjective, noun*

fortune *noun* fortunes

forward *noun* forwards

forwards *adverb*

fossil *noun* fossils

fountain *noun* fountains

fox *noun* foxes

fox *verb* foxes, foxing, foxed

frame *noun* frames

frame *verb* frames, framing, framed

frantic *adjective*

frantically *adverb*

> Watch out! To make **frantic** into an adverb you add -**ally**: **frantic** + **ally**.

fraught *adjective*

free *adjective* freer, freest

free *verb* frees, freeing, freed

freedom *noun*

freeze *verb* freezes, freezing, froze, frozen

frequency *noun* frequencies

frequent *verb* frequents, frequenting, frequented

fresh *adjective* fresher, freshest

friend *noun* friends

> Watch Out! There is an **i** in **friend**. Try 'I am a friend' to help you remember it.

fright *noun* frights

frighten *verb* frightens, frightening, frightened

frog *noun* frogs

a b c d e **f** g h i j k l m n o p q r s t u v w x y z

★ **Flour** is powder used in making bread. A **flower** is a part of a plant.

✪ **Flu** is an illness. A **flue** is a pipe for smoke and fumes. **Flew** is the past of fly.

☆ You use **for** in phrases like *a present for you*. You use **fore** in phrases like *come to the fore*.

✤ You use **forever** in e.g. *They are forever complaining*. You can also use **for ever** in e.g. *The rain seemed to go on for ever*.

A B C D E F G H I J K L M N O P Q R S T U V W X Y Z

from *preposition*

front *noun* fronts

frost *noun* frosts

frost *verb* frosts, frosting, frosted

frown *verb* frowns, frowning, frowned

frown *noun* frowns

fruit *noun* fruit or fruits

Watch out! The 'oo' sound is made with **ui** in **fruit**.

fry *verb* fries, frying, fried

fudge *noun*

fuel *noun* fuels

fuel *verb* fuels, fuelling, fuelled

full *adjective, adverb*

fun *noun*

funny *adjective* funnier, funniest

fur *noun* furs

furious *adjective*

furiously *adverb*

furniture *noun*

further *verb* furthers, furthering, furthered

fury *noun* furies

fuss *noun* fusses

fuss *verb* fusses, fussing, fussed

future *noun*

Gg

gain *verb* gains, gaining, gained

gain *noun* gains

gallery *noun* galleries

gallop *noun* gallops

gallop *verb* gallops, galloping, galloped

game *noun* games

gang *noun* gangs

gang *verb* gangs, ganging, ganged

gap *noun* gaps

gape *verb* gapes, gaping, gaped

garage *noun* garages

garden *noun* gardens

gardener *noun* gardeners

gardening *noun*

gas *noun* gases

gas *verb* gasses, gassing, gassed

gasp *verb* gasps, gasping, gasped

gate *noun* gates

gateau *noun* gateaux

Gateau is a French word. It means 'a rich cream cake'.

gather *verb* gathers, gathering, gathered

gay *adjective* gayer, gayest

gaze *verb* gazes, gazing, gazed

gaze *noun* gazes

gem *noun* gems

general *noun* generals

generally *adverb*

gentle *adjective* gentler, gentlest

gentleman *noun* gentlemen

gentlemanly *adjective*

gently *adverb*

genuine *adjective*

genus *noun* genera

germ *noun* germs

germinate *verb* germinates, germinating, germinated

gesture *noun* gestures

get *verb* gets, getting, got

ghost *noun* ghosts

Watch out! There is a silent **h** in **ghost**.

giant *noun* giants

gift *noun* gifts

giggle *verb* giggles, giggling, giggled

giggle *noun* giggles

ginger *noun*

giraffe *noun* giraffes

girl *noun* girls

give *verb* gives, giving, gave, given

glad *adjective* gladder, gladdest

glamorous *adjective*

glance *verb* glances, glancing, glanced

glance *noun* glances

glare *verb* glares, glaring, glared

glare *noun* glares

glass *noun* glasses

gleam *noun* gleams

gleam *verb* gleams, gleaming, gleamed

gleeful *adjective*

glide *verb* glides, gliding, glided

glimpse *verb* glimpses, glimpsing, glimpsed

glimpse *noun* glimpses

glisten *verb* glistens, glistening, glistened

glitter *verb* glitters, glittering, glittered

Gg: Try also words beginning with **gh-** or **gu-**

globally adverb

gloom noun

gloominess noun

glorious adjective

gloriously adverb

glory noun glories

glove noun gloves

glow verb glows, glowing, glowed

glue noun glues

glue verb glues, gluing, glued

gluey adjective

gnarled adjective

Watch out! There is a silent **g** in **gnarled**, **gnash**, **gnat**, **gnaw** and **gnome**.

gnat noun gnats

gnaw verb gnaws, gnawing, gnawed

go verb goes, going, went, gone

Watch out! **Going** is spelt **go** + **ing**, **going**.

go noun goes

goal noun goals

goat noun goats

goddess noun goddesses

Double up! There is double **d** and double **s** in **goddess**.

goes verb

Watch out! There is an **e** in **goes**, **go** + **es** = **goes**

gold noun

golden adjective

good adjective better, best

goodbye interjection

goodness noun

gorgeously adverb

government noun governments

gown noun gowns

grab verb grabs, grabbing, grabbed

Watch Out! Double the **b** in **grab** when you add **-ing** or **-ed**, **grabbing**, **grabbed**.

gradual adjective

gradually adverb

grain noun grains

grainy adjective

grammar noun grammars

Watch out! **Grammar** ends in **-ar**.

grand adjective grander, grandest

grandfather noun grandfathers

grandmother noun grandmothers

granite noun

grant verb grants, granting, granted

grant noun grants

grasp verb grasps, grasping, grasped

grass noun grasses

grate noun grates

grate verb grates, grating, grated

grateful adjective

grave noun graves

grave adjective graver, gravest

gravel noun

gravely adverb

gravity noun

great adjective greater, greatest

greatly adjective

green adjective greener, greenest

green noun greens

greet verb greets, greeting, greeted

grenade noun grenades

grey adjective greyer, greyest

grief noun

grim adjective grimmer, grimmest

grin noun grins

grin verb grins, grinning, grinned

grind verb grinds, grinding, ground

grip verb grips, gripping, gripped

grip noun grips

groan verb groans, groaning, groaned

groan noun groans

grotesquely adverb

ground

group noun groups

group verb groups, grouping, grouped

grow verb grows, growing, grew, grown

growl verb growls, growling, growled

growl noun growls

grown verb

a
b
c
d
e
f
g
h
i
j
k
l
m
n
o
p
q
r
s
t
u
v
w
x
y
z

A
B
C
D
E
F
G
H
I
J
K
L
M
N
O
P
Q
R
S
T
U
V
W
X
Y
Z

grumble *verb* grumbles, grumbling, grumbled

grunt *verb* grunts, grunting, grunted

grunt *noun* grunts

guarantee *noun* guarantees

guarantee *verb* guarantees, guaranteeing, guaranteed

guard *verb* guards, guarding, guarded

guard *noun* guards

Watch out! There is a silent **u** in **guard**.

guardianship *noun*

guess *noun* guesses

guess *verb* guesses, guessing, guessed

guesswork *noun*

guest *noun* guests

guide *noun* guides

guide *verb* guides, guiding, guided

guilty *adjective* guiltier, guiltiest

guitarist *noun*

gulp *verb* gulps, gulping, gulped

gulp *noun* gulps

gun *noun* guns

gun *verb* guns, gunning, gunned

guy *noun* guys or guy-ropes

gym *noun* gyms

Hh

habit *noun* habits

hadn't

Tip! **Hadn't** = **had** + **not**. Add an **apostrophe** between the **n** and **t**.

hairy *adjective* hairier, hairiest

half *noun* halves

Watch out! The plural of **half** is **halves**.

halfway *adverb*, *adjective*

hall *noun* halls

halt *verb* halts, halting, halted

halve *verb* halves, halving, halved

hammer *noun* hammers

hammer *verb* hammers, hammering, hammered

hand *noun* hands

hand *verb* hands, handing, handed

handful *noun* handfuls

handkerchief *noun* handkerchiefs

handle *noun* handles

handle *verb* handles, handling, handled

handsome *adjective* handsomer, handsomest

hang *verb* hangs, hanging, hung

happen *verb* happens, happening, happened

Tip! To make the past tense, start with **happen** and add **-ed**, **happened**.

happily *adverb*

Tip! Change the **-y** to **i** in **happy** and add **–ly**, **happily**.

happiness *noun*

happy *adjective* happier, happiest

Tip! Change the **-y** to **i** in **happy** and add **-ier** or **–iest**, **happier**, **happiest**.

happy-go-lucky *adjective*

harass *verb* harasses, harassing, harassed

Watch out! There is only one **r** in **harass**.

hardly *adverb*

hare *noun* hares

harm *verb* harms, harming, harmed

harness *noun* harnesses

harness *verb* harnesses, harnessing, harnessed

harsh *adjective* harsher, harshest

hasn't

Tip! **Hasn't** = **has** + **not**. Add an **apostrophe** between the **n** and **t**.

haste *noun*

hasten *verb* hastens, hastening, hastened

hat *noun* hats

hatch *noun* hatches

hatch *verb* hatches, hatching, hatched

hate *verb* hates, hating, hated

hate *noun* hates

haughty *adjective* haughtier, haughtiest

haul *verb* hauls, hauling, hauled

haul *noun* hauls

haunt *verb* haunts, haunting, haunted

have *verb* has, having, had

haven't

Tip! **Haven't** = **have** + **not**. Add an **apostrophe** between the **n** and **t**.

hay *noun*

he *pronoun, noun*

he'd

Tip! **He'd** = **he** + **would** or **had**. Add an **apostrophe** between the **e** and **d**.

he'll

Tip! **He'll** = **he** + **will**. Add an **apostrophe** between the **e** and **l**.

he's

Tip! **He's** = **he** + **is** or **has**. Add an **apostrophe** between the **e** and **s**.

head *noun* heads

head *verb* heads, heading, headed

health *noun*

healthy *adjective* healthier, healthiest

heap *noun* heaps

heap *verb* heaps, heaping, heaped

hear★ *verb* hears, hearing, heard

Watch out! The past tense of **hear** is **heard**.

hearing *noun* hearings

heart *noun* hearts

hearty *adjective* heartier, heartiest

heat *noun* heats

heat *verb* heats, heating, heated

heave *verb* heaves, heaving, heaved

heaven *noun*

heavily *adverb*

heaviness *noun*

hedge *noun* hedges

hedge *verb* hedges, hedging, hedged

heel *noun* heels

heel *verb* heels, heeling, heeled

height *noun* heights

Watch out! **Height** has a tricky bit in the middle, **eigh**.

heighten *verb* heightens, heightening, heightened

helicopter *noun* helicopters

hello *interjection*

helmet *noun* helmets

help *verb* helps, helping, helped

help *noun* helps

helpless *adjective*

hen *noun* hens

her *pronoun, determiner*

herd *noun* herds

herd *verb* herds, herding, herded

here *adverb*

hero *noun* heroes

Watch out! The plural of **hero** is **heroes**.

hers *pronoun*

Watch out! You use **hers** in, *the book is hers*. There is no apostrophe in this word.

herself *pronoun*

hesitancy *noun*

hesitant *adjective*

hesitate *verb* hesitates, hesitating, hesitated

hesitation *noun*

hide *verb* hides, hiding, hid, hidden

high *adjective* higher, highest

highlands *plural noun*

highly *adverb*

hike *noun* hikes

hike *verb* hikes, hiking, hiked

hiker *noun*

him *pronoun*

himself *pronoun*

hindrance *noun*

hint *noun* hints

hint *verb* hints, hinting, hinted

hip *noun* hips

hire *verb* hires, hiring, hired

his *determiner, pronoun*

hiss *verb* hisses, hissing, hissed

a b c d e f g h i j k l m n o p q r s t u v w x y z

★ To **hear** is to listen. You use **here** in, e.g. *come here*.

Hh: Try also words beginning with **wh-**

A B C D E F G H I J K L M N O P Q R S T U V W X Y Z

historic *adjective*

history *noun* histories

hit *verb* hits, hitting, hit

hit *noun* hits

hoarder *noun*

hoax *noun* hoaxes

hoax *verb* hoaxes, hoaxing, hoaxed

hold *verb* holds, holding, held

hold *noun* holds

hole★ *noun* holes

hollow *verb* hollows, hollowing, hollowed

hollow *noun* hollows

holy *adjective* holier, holiest

home *noun* homes

home *verb* homes, homing, homed

homeliness *noun*

homesickness *noun*

honest *adjective*

honey *noun*

honeysuckle *noun*

honour *noun* honours

honour *verb* honours, honouring, honoured

honourable *adjective*

honourably *adverb*

hoody *noun* hoodies

hoof *noun* hoofs or hooves

hook *noun* hooks

hook *verb* hooks, hooking, hooked

hop *verb* hops, hopping, hopped

hop *noun* hops

hope *noun* hopes

hope *verb* hopes, hoping, hoped

hopeless *adjective*

horizon *noun* horizons

horn *noun* horns

horrible *adjective*

horrid *adjective*

horrifically *adverb*

horrify *verb* horrifies, horrifying, horrified

horror *noun* horrors

horse *noun* horses

horsemanship *noun*

hospitably *adverb*

hospital *noun* hospitals

host *noun* hosts

hot *adjective* hotter, hottest

hotel *noun* hotels

hound *noun* hounds

hound *verb* hounds, hounding, hounded

hour *noun* hours

house *noun* houses

house *verb* houses, housing, housed

household *noun* households

hover *verb* hovers, hovering, hovered

hovercraft *noun* hovercraft

how *adverb*

however *adverb*, *conjunction*

howl *noun* howls

howl *verb* howls, howling, howled

huddle *verb* huddles, huddling, huddled

hug *verb* hugs, hugging, hugged

hug *noun* hugs

huge *adjective* huger, hugest

hum *verb* hums, humming, hummed

hum *noun* hums

human *noun* humans

humbly *adverb*

humidity *noun*

humility *noun*

humorous *adjective*

hunger *noun*

hungry *adjective* hungrier, hungriest

hunk *noun* hunks

hunt *verb* hunts, hunting, hunted

hunt *noun* hunts

hunter *noun* hunters or huntsmen

hurl *verb* hurls, hurling, hurled

hurricane *noun* hurricanes

hurry *verb* hurries, hurrying, hurried

hurt *verb* hurts, hurting, hurt

> Watch out! The past tense of **hurt** is **hurt**.

hurtful *adjective*

husband *noun* husbands

husky *adjective* huskier, huskiest

husky *noun* huskies

hut *noun* huts

★ A **hole** is a gap or opening. You use **whole** in, e.g. *I saw the whole film.*

Ii

I'd

Watch Out! **I'd = I + would.**
Add an **apostrophe** between
the **I** and **d.**

I'll

Watch Out! **I'll = I + will.** Add
an **apostrophe** between the
I and **ll.**

I'm

Watch Out! **I'm = I + am.** Add
an **apostrophe** between the
I and **m.**

I've

Watch Out! **I've = I + have.**
Add an **apostrophe** between
the **I** and **v.**

ice *noun* ices

ice *verb* ices, icing, iced

icy *adjective* icier, iciest

idea *noun* ideas

identify *verb* identifies,
identifying, identified

idiot *noun* idiots

idiotically *adverb*

if *conjunction*

ignore *verb* ignores, ignoring,
ignored

ill *adjective, adverb*

illegible *adjective*

illuminations *plural noun*

illustrate *verb* illustrates,
illustrating, illustrated

imagination *noun*
imaginations

imagine *verb* imagines,
imagining, imagined

imitate *verb* imitates,
imitating, imitated

immature *adjective*

immediate *adjective*

immediately *adverb*

immense *adjective*

immortal *adjective*

impatient *adjective*

impatiently *adverb*

imperfect *adjective*

impish *adjective*

important *adjective*

impossibility *noun*

impossible *adjective*

impress *verb* impresses,
impressing, impressed

impression *noun* impressions

imprison *verb* imprisons,
imprisoning, imprisoned

improve *verb* improves,
improving, improved

in *preposition, adverb*

Watch out! Phrases like **in
front**, **in case** or **in fact** are
two separate words.

inactive *adjective*

inch *noun* inches

include *verb* includes,
including, included

incorporate *verb* incorporates,
incorporating, incorporated

incorporation *noun*

incorrect *adjective*

increase *verb* increases,
increasing, increased

increase *noun* increases

incredible *adjective*

indeed *adverb*

independence *noun*

independent *adjective*

independently *noun*

index *noun* indexes

indicate *verb* indicates,
indicating, indicated

industry *noun* industries

infectious *adjective*

inferior *noun* inferiors

inferiority *noun*

inflate *verb* inflates, inflating,
inflated

inflation *noun*

influence *noun* influences

influence *verb* influences,
influencing, influenced

information *noun*

inhabitant *noun* inhabitants

injection *noun*

injure *verb* injures, injuring,
injured

inn *noun* inns

inner *adjective*

innocence *noun*

innocent *adjective*

inquire *verb* inquires, inquiring,
inquired

insect *noun* insects

inside *noun* insides

insignificance *noun*

insist *verb* insists, insisting,
insisted

a
b
c
d
e
f
g
h
i
j
k
l
m
n
o
p
q
r
s
t
u
v
w
x
y
z

A B C D E F G H I J K L M N O P Q R S T U V W X Y Z

insistence *noun*

instant *noun* instants

instantly *adverb*

instead *adverb*

instruction *noun* instructions

instrument *noun* instruments

insult *verb* insults, insulting, insulted

insult *noun* insults

intellectually *adverb*

intend *verb* intends, intending, intended

interest *verb* interests, interesting, interested

interest *noun* interests

Watch out! There is an **er** in the middle of **interest**, **int-er-est**.

interfere *verb* interferes, interfering, interfered

internally *adverb*

interrupt *verb* interrupts, interrupting, interrupted

interview *noun* interviews

interview *verb* interviews, interviewing, interviewed

into *preposition*

introduce *verb* introduces, introducing, introduced

invade *verb* invades, invading, invaded

invasion *noun* invasions

invent *verb* invents, inventing, invented

invention *noun*

inventor *noun*

investigate *verb* investigates, investigating, investigated

investigator *noun*

invisible *adjective*

invite *verb* invites, inviting, invited

involve *verb* involves, involving, involved

iron *noun* irons

iron *verb* irons, ironing, ironed

irregular *adjective*

irregularly *adverb*

irrelevant *adjective*

irresponsible *adjective*

irritability *noun*

irritant *noun*

island *noun* islands

isle *noun* isles

isn't

Watch Out! **Isn't** = **is** + **not**. Add an **apostrophe** between the **n** and **t**.

issue *verb* issues, issuing, issued

issue *noun* issues

it'll

Watch Out! **It'll** = **it** + **will**. Add an **apostrophe** between the **t** and **l**.

it's

Watch out! **It's** = **it** + **is**. Add an **apostrophe** between the **t** and **s**.

itchy *adjective* itchier, itchiest

item *noun* items

its *determiner, pronoun*

Watch out! **Its** is different from **it's**. **Its** does **not** mean **it is**.

itself *pronoun*

Jj

jacket *noun* jackets

jam *noun* jams

jam *verb* jams, jamming, jammed

jar *noun* jars

jar *verb* jars, jarring, jarred

jaw *noun* jaws

jealous *adjective*

Watch out! **Jealous** begins with **jea**.

jealously *adverb*

jelly *noun* jellies

jerk *verb* jerks, jerking, jerked

jerk *noun* jerks

jet *verb* jets, jetting, jetted

jewel *noun* jewels

job *noun* jobs

jogger *noun*

join *verb* joins, joining, joined

join *noun* joins

joke *noun* jokes

joke *verb* jokes, joking, joked

jolly *adjective* jollier, jolliest

jolly *verb* jollies, jollying, jollied

journey *noun, verb* journeys, journeying, journeyed

joyful *adjective*

Kk: Try also words beginning with **c-**, **ch-**, or **qu-**

judge *noun* judges

judge *verb* judges, judging, judged

juice *noun* juices

> Watch out! The 'oo' sound is spelt with **ui** and the 's' sound is spelt with a **c**, **juice**.

jump *verb* jumps, jumping, jumped

jump *noun* jumps

junction *noun* junctions

jungle *noun* jungles

junior *noun* juniors

jury *noun* juries

just *adjective, adverb*

Kk

keen *adjective* keener, keenest

keep *verb* keeps, keeping, kept

> Watch out! The past tense of **keep** is **kept**.

keep *noun* keeps

kettle *noun* kettles

key★ *noun* keys

kick *verb* kicks, kicking, kicked

kick *noun* kicks

kid *noun* kids

kid *verb* kids, kidding, kidded

kidnap *verb* kidnaps, kidnapping, kidnapped

kill *verb* kills, killing, killed

kind *noun* kinds

kind *adjective* kinder, kindest

kindly *adjective* kindlier, kindliest

kindness *adjective*

king *noun* kings

kiss *noun* kisses

kiss *verb* kisses, kissing, kissed

kit *noun* kits

kitchen *noun* kitchens

kite *noun* kites

kitten *noun* kittens

knead✿ *verb* kneads, kneading, kneaded

knee *noun* knees

kneel *verb* kneels, kneeling, knelt

knife *noun* knives

> Watch out! Most nouns ending in **fe** have plurals ending in **ves**, e.g. **knife – knives**

knife *verb* knifes, knifing, knifed

knock *verb* knocks, knocking, knocked

knock *noun* knocks

knot *noun* knots

knot *verb* knots, knotting, knotted

know *verb* knows, knowing, knew, known

knowledge *noun*

> Watch out! **Knowledge** has a silent **k** and the 'j' sound is spelt **-dge**.

knuckle *noun* knuckles

Ll

label *noun* labels

label *verb* labels, labelling, labelled

lace *noun* laces

lace *verb* laces, lacing, laced

lack *verb* lacks, lacking, lacked

lad *noun* lads

ladder *noun* ladders

lady *noun* ladies

lake *noun* lakes

lamb *noun* lambs

lamp *noun* lamps

land *noun* lands

land *verb* lands, landing, landed

landing *noun* landings

landscape *noun* landscapes

lane *noun* lanes

language *noun* languages

lantern *noun* lanterns

lap *noun* laps

lap *verb* laps, lapping, lapped

laptop *noun* laptops

large *adjective* larger, largest

largeness *noun*

lash *noun* lashes

lash *verb* lashes, lashing, lashed

last *verb* lasts, lasting, lasted

late *adjective, adverb* later, latest

lateness *noun*

a b c d e f g h i **j k l** m n o p q r s t u v w x y z

★ A **key** is a device for opening a lock. A **quay** is a place where ships tie up.

✿ To **knead** is to work a mixture into a dough. To **need** is to require something.

A B C D E F G H I J K L M N O P Q R S T U V W X Y Z

laugh *verb* laughs, laughing, laughed

laugh *noun* laughs

laughter *noun*

launch *verb* launches, launching, launched

launch *noun* launches

law *noun* laws

lawyer *noun* lawyers

lay *verb* lays, laying, laid

> Watch out! The past tense of **lay** is **laid**.

layer *noun* layers

laze *verb* lazes, lazing, lazed

laziness *noun*

lazy *adjective* lazier, laziest

lead *verb* leads, leading, led

> Watch out! The past tense of **lead** is **led**.

lead *noun* leads

leader *noun* leaders

leaf *noun* leaves

league *noun* leagues

leakage *noun*

lean *verb* leans, leaning, leaned or leant

lean *adjective* leaner, leanest

leap *noun* leaps

leap *verb* leaps, leaping, leapt or leaped

> Watch out! The past tense of **leap** is **leapt**.

learn *verb* learns, learning, learnt or learned

least *determiner, adverb, pronoun*

leather *noun* leathers

leave *verb* leaves, leaving, left

> Watch out! The past tense of **leave** is **left**.

lecture *noun* lectures

lecture *verb* lectures, lecturing, lectured

lecturer *noun*

ledge *noun* ledges

leek *noun* leeks

leg *noun* legs

legacy *noun* legacies

legend *noun* legends

legible *adjective*

leisure *noun*

lend *verb* lends, lending, lent

length *noun* lengths

> Watch out! There is a silent **g** in **length**.

leniency *noun*

lenient *adjective*

lens *noun* lenses

less *determiner, adverb, pronoun, preposition*

lesson *noun* lessons

let *verb* lets, letting, let

> Watch out! The past tense of **let** is **let**.

let's *verb*

> Watch Out! **Let's** = **let** + **us**. Add an **apostrophe** between the **t** and **s**.

letter *noun* letters

level *verb* levels, levelling, levelled

level *noun* levels

lever *noun* levers

library *noun* libraries

licence★ *noun* licences

license★ *verb* licenses, licensing, licensed

lick *verb* licks, licking, licked

lick *noun* licks

lid *noun* lids

lie *verb* lies, lying, lied

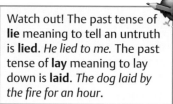

> Watch out! The past tense of **lie** meaning to tell an untruth is **lied**. *He lied to me.* The past tense of **lay** meaning to lay down is **laid**. *The dog laid by the fire for an hour.*

lie *noun* lies

life *noun* lives

lift *verb* lifts, lifting, lifted

lift *noun* lifts

lift-off *noun* lift-offs

light *noun* lights

light *adjective* lighter, lightest

light *verb* lights, lighting, lit or lighted

lightly *adverb*

★ **Licence** is a noun and **license** is a verb, *a TV licence, The ship is licensed to carry passengers.*

lightning noun

Watch out! **Lightning has** no **e** in the middle.

like verb likes, liking, liked

likeable adjective

likely adjective likelier, likeliest

limb noun limbs

limitation noun

limitless adjective

line noun lines

line verb lines, lining, lined

linger verb lingers, lingering, lingered

link noun links

link verb links, linking, linked

lion noun lions

list noun lists

list verb lists, listing, listed

listen verb listens, listening, listened

little determiner, adjective less, least

live verb lives, living, lived

lively adjective livelier, liveliest

load noun loads

Watch out! The long vowel 'o' is spelt **oa** in **load**.

load verb loads, loading, loaded

long adjective longer, longest

long adverb longer, longest

long verb longs, longing, longed

look verb looks, looking, looked

look noun looks

loose★ adjective looser, loosest

lose verb loses, losing, lost

Watch out! The past tense of **lose** is **lost**.

lot noun lots

Watch out! **A lot** is two words, not one. Keep them apart!

love noun loves

love verb loves, loving, loved

lovely adjective lovelier, loveliest

Tip! **Lovely** is spelt **love + ly**, **lovely**.

lucky adjective luckier, luckiest

Mm

machine noun machines

mad adjective madder, maddest

magazine noun magazines

magic noun

magical adjective

magician noun magicians

magnet noun magnets

magnetic adjective

magnification noun

magnificent adjective

magnificently adverb

maid noun maids

maiden noun maidens

mail verb mails, mailing, mailed

main adjective, noun

mainly adverb

majestically adverb

majesty noun majesties

major noun majors

majority noun majorities

make verb makes, making, made

Watch out! The past tense of **make** is **made**.

make noun makes

male noun males

malicious adjective

mammal noun mammals

man noun men

man verb mans, manning, manned

manage verb manages, managing, managed

manageable adjective

mane noun manes

manliness noun

manner noun manners

manually adverb

manufacture verb manufactures, manufacturing, manufactured

manure noun

many determiner more, most

map noun maps

map verb maps, mapping, mapped

marble noun marbles

march verb marches, marching, marched

march noun marches

mark noun marks

a b c d e f g h i j k l m n o p q r s t u v w x y z

★ **Loose** is different from **lose**, which is a verb. *We have no time to lose.*

A
B
C
D
E
F
G
H
I
J
K
L
M
N
O
P
Q
R
S
T
U
V
W
X
Y
Z

mark *verb* marks, marking, marked

market *noun* markets

market *verb* markets, marketing, marketed

marriage *noun* marriages

marry *verb* marries, marrying, married

marsh *noun* marshes

marvellous *adjective*

marvellously *adverb*

mask *noun* masks

mask *verb* masks, masking, masked

mass *noun* masses

mass *verb* masses, massing, massed

massive *adjective*

master *noun* masters

master *verb* masters, mastering, mastered

mat *noun* mats

matador *noun* matadors

match *noun* matches

match *verb* matches, matching, matched

mate *noun* mates

mate *verb* mates, mating, mated

material *noun* materials

maternal *adjective*

mathematician *noun* mathematicians

matt *adjective*

matter *noun* matters

matter *verb* matters, mattering, mattered

may *verb* might

maybe *adverb*

me *pronoun*

meadow *noun* meadows

meal *noun*

mean *verb* means, meaning, meant

> Watch Out! The 'ee' sound is spelt **ea** and the past tense of **mean** is **meant**.

meanwhile *adverb*

measure *verb* measures, measuring, measured

measure *noun* measures

meat *noun* meats

medal *noun* medals

meddle *verb* meddles, meddling, meddled

meddlesome *adjective*

median *noun* medians

medically *adverb*

medicinal *adjective*

medicine *noun* medicines

medium *noun* media or mediums

> Watch out! There is an **i** in **medium**.

meet *verb* meets, meeting, met

> Watch out! The past tense of **meet** is **met**.

meeting *noun* meetings

melt *verb* melts, melting, melted

memory *noun* memories

mend *verb* mends, mending, mended

mention *verb* mentions, mentioning, mentioned

> Watch out! The 'shun' sound is spelt **-tion** in **mention**.

mention *noun* mentions

merchant *noun* merchants

mercilessly *adverb*

mercy *noun* mercies

mere *noun* meres

merely *adverb*

merry *adjective* merrier, merriest

mess *noun* messes

mess *verb* messes, messing, messed

message *noun* messages

messenger *noun* messengers

messily *adverb*

metal *noun* metals

meter *noun* meters

middle *noun* middles

midnight *noun*

midst *noun*

mighty *adjective* mightier, mightiest

militaristic *adjective*

military *adjective*

milk *verb* milks, milking, milked

million *noun* millions

millionaire *noun* millionaires

> Double up the **l** in **millionaire** but the **n** stays single.

mind *noun* minds

mind *verb* minds, minding, minded

mine *noun* mines

mine *verb* mines, mining, mined

mineral *noun* minerals

minister *noun* ministers

minor *adjective*

minority *noun* minorities

minute *noun* minutes

> Watch out! There is **no** mini in **minute**. Remember it is **min + ute**.

minutely *adverb*

miracle *noun* miracles

mirror *noun* mirrors

misbehave *verb* misbehaves, misbehaving, misbehaved

mischief *noun*

mischievous *adjective*

miser *noun* misers

miserable *adjective*

miserly *adjective*

misery *noun* miseries

mislead *verb* misleads, misleading, misled

miss *verb* misses, missing, missed

miss *noun* misses

mission *noun* missions

misspell *verb* misspells, misspelling, misspelt or misspelled

mist *noun* mists

mistake *noun* mistakes

mistake *verb* mistakes, mistaking, mistook, mistaken

mix *verb* mixes, mixing, mixed

mixture *noun* mixtures

moan *noun* moans

moan *verb* moans, moaning, moaned

mobile *noun* mobiles

mobility *noun*

model *noun* models

model *verb* models, modelling, modelled

modern *adjective*

modernize *verb* modernizes, modernizing, modernized

modest *adjective*

modification *noun*

moisten *verb* moistens, moistening, moistened

moisture *noun*

moment *noun* moments

money *noun*

monk *noun* monks

monkey *noun* monkeys

monster *noun* monsters

month *noun* months

mood *noun* moods

moon *noun* moons

moonlight *noun*

moor *noun* moors

moor *verb* moors, mooring, moored

more *determiner, pronoun, adverb*

morning *noun* mornings

mortal *adjective*

mortally *adverb*

mosque *noun* mosques

mosquito *noun* mosquitoes

moss *noun* mosses

most *determiner, pronoun, adverb*

mostly *adverb*

moth *noun* moths

mother *noun* mothers

motion *noun* motions

motor *noun* motors

mound *noun* mounds

mount *verb* mounts, mounting, mounted

mount *noun* mounts

mountain *noun* mountains

mountainous *adjective*

mourner *noun*

mourning *verb*

mouth *noun* mouths

move *verb* moves, moving, moved

move *noun* moves

movement *noun* movements

much *adjective, pronoun, adverb*

mud *noun*

muddy *adjective* muddier, muddiest

muffle *verb* muffles, muffling, muffled

multiply *verb* multiplies, multiplying, multiplied

multiracial *adjective*

mum *noun* mums

mumble *verb* mumbles, mumbling, mumbled

murder *verb* murders, murdering, murdered

murder *noun* murders

murmur *noun* murmurs

murmur *verb* murmurs, murmuring, murmured

a
b
c
d
e
f
g
h
i
j
k
l
m
n
o
p
q
r
s
t
u
v
w
x
y
z

Nn: Try also words beginning with **gn-**, or **kn-**

A B C D E F G H I J K L **M** N O P Q R S T U V W X Y Z

muscle *noun* muscles

Watch out! There is an **sc** in **muscle**.

muscle *verb* muscles, muscling, muscled

museum *noun* museums

music *noun*

musically *adverb*

musician *noun* musicians

must *verb*

mustiness *noun*

mutter *verb* mutters, muttering, muttered

my *determiner*

myself *pronoun*

mysterious *adjective*

mystery *noun* mysteries

myth *noun* myths

Nn

nail *noun* nails

nail *verb* nails, nailing, nailed

name *noun* names

name *verb* names, naming, named

narrate *verb* narrates, narrating, narrated

narration *noun*

narrow *adjective* narrower, narrowest

nasty *adjective* nastier, nastiest

nation *noun* nations

national *adjective*

native *noun* natives

natural *noun* naturals

naturally *adverb*

nature *noun* natures

near *adverb*, *adjective* nearer, nearest

near *verb* nears, nearing, neared

nearby *adjective*

nearly *adverb*

neat *adjective* neater, neatest

neatly *adverb*

necessarily *adverb*

necessary *adjective*

Watch out! There is a **single c** and a **double s** in **necessary**.

neck *noun* necks

need★ *verb* needs, needing, needed

need *noun* needs

needle *noun* needles

negotiations *plural noun*

neighbour *noun* neighbours

neighbouring *adjective*

neither *determiner*, *pronoun*, *conjunction*

nephew *noun* nephews

nervous *adjective*

nervously *adverb*

nest *noun* nests

nest *verb* nests, nesting, nested

net *noun* nets

neuter *verb* neuters, neutering, neutered

never *adverb*

new *adjective* newer, newest

newness *noun*

news *noun*

newspaper *noun* newspapers

next *adjective*, *adverb*

nice *adjective* nicer, nicest

night *noun* nights

nightmare *noun* nightmares

no *interjection*, *determiner*, *adverb*

no one *pronoun*

Watch Out! **No one** is two separate words.

noble *adjective* nobler, noblest

noble *noun* nobles

nobly *adverb*

nobody *noun* nobodies

nod *verb* nods, nodding, nodded

noise *noun* noises

noisy *adjective* noisier, noisiest

none✪ *pronoun*, *adverb*

nonsense *noun*

noon *noun*

nor *conjunction*

normal *adjective*

normality *noun*

normally *adverb*

north *noun*, *adjective*, *adverb*

northern *adjective*

nose *noun* noses

nose *verb* noses, nosing, nosed

nostril *noun* nostrils

not *adverb*

notably *adverb*

note *noun* notes

★ To **need** is to require something. To **knead** is to work a mixture into a dough.
✪ You use **none** in, e.g. *none of us*. A **nun** is a member of a convent.

Nn: Try also words beginning with gn-, or kn-

note *verb* notes, noting, noted

nothing *noun*

notice *noun* notices

notice *verb* notices, noticing, noticed

noticeable *adjective*

nought *noun* noughts

now *adverb, conjunction, noun*

nowhere *adverb*

nudge *verb* nudges, nudging, nudged

nuisance *noun* nuisances

> Watch out! There is a **ui** in the middle of **nuisance**.

number *noun* numbers

number *verb* numbers, numbering, numbered

numbness *noun*

nurse *noun* nurses

nurse *verb* nurses, nursing, nursed

nut *noun* nuts

nutrition *noun*

nutritious *adjective*

Oo

oak *noun* oaks

oar★ *noun* oars

obedience *noun*

obedient *adjective*

obey *verb* obeys, obeying, obeyed

object *noun* objects

object *verb* objects, objecting, objected

obligatory *adjective*

oblige *verb* obliges, obliging, obliged

observance *noun* observances

observant *adjective*

observantly *adverb*

observation *noun* observations

observe *verb* observes, observing, observed

obvious *adjective*

obviously *adverb*

occasion *noun* occasions

occupy *verb* occupies, occupying, occupied

occur *verb* occurs, occurring, occurred

ocean *noun* oceans

odd *adjective* odder, oddest

oddness *noun*

odorous *adjective*

odour *noun* odours

of✪ *preposition*

off✪ *adverb, preposition*

offence *noun* offences

office *noun* offices

officer *noun* officers

official *noun* officials

often *adverb*

oh *interjection*

oil *noun* oils

oil *verb* oils, oiling, oiled

old *adjective* older, oldest

omission *noun* omissions

omit *verb* omits, omitting, omitted

on *preposition, adverb*

once *adverb, conjunction*

one☆ *noun* ones

only *adjective, adverb, conjunction*

onto *preposition*

open *verb* opens, opening, opened

> Tip! Start with **open** and add **-ed**, open + ed = **opened**.

operate *verb* operates, operating, operated

operatic *adjective*

opinion *noun* opinions

opponent *noun* opponents

opportunity *noun* opportunities

opposite *noun* opposites

or *conjunction*

orange *noun* oranges

orbit *noun* orbits

orbit *verb* orbits, orbiting, orbited

orbital *adjective*

orchard *noun* orchards

order *noun* orders

order *verb* orders, ordering, ordered

orderliness *noun*

ordinary *adjective*

a b c d e f g h i j k l m n o p q r s t u v w x y z

★ An **oar** is used for a rowing boat. You use **or** in, e.g. *Do you want a cake or a biscuit.* **Ore** is rock with metal in it.
✪ **Of** is different from **off**. *I've never heard of it. He fell off his bike.*
☆ **One** is a number. One also refers to a person or thing. **Won** is the past tense of to win.

A B C D E F G H I J K L M N O P Q R S T U V W X Y Z

organize *verb* organizes, organizing, organized

Tip! You can spell this **-ize** or **-ise**.

origin *noun* origins

original *adjective*

originator *noun*

other *pronoun* others

otherwise *adverb*

ought *verb*

ours *pronoun*

Watch out! There is no apostrophe in **ours**.

ourselves *pronoun*

out *adverb*

outer *adjective*

outrageous *adjective*

outside *noun* outsides

oven *noun* ovens

over *noun* overs

overalls *plural noun*

overcome *verb* overcomes, overcoming, overcame, overcome

overhead *adjective, adverb*

owl *noun* owls

own *verb* owns, owning, owned

owner *noun* owners

oxygen *noun*

Pp

pace *noun* paces

pace *verb* paces, pacing, paced

pack *noun* packs

pack *verb* packs, packing, packed

packet *noun* packets

pad *noun* pads

pad *verb* pads, padding, padded

paddle *verb* paddles, paddling, paddled

paddle *noun* paddles

page *noun* pages

pageant *noun* pageants

pail★ *noun* pails

pain *noun* pains

pain✪ *verb* pains, paining, pained

painful *adjective*

paint *noun* paints

paint *verb* paints, painting, painted

painting *noun* paintings

pair☆ *noun* pairs

palace *noun* palaces

pale *adjective* paler, palest

palm *noun* palms

palm *verb* palms, palming, palmed

pan *noun* pans

panel *noun* panels

panic *verb* panics, panicking, panicked

pant *verb* pants, panting, panted

paper *noun* papers

paper *verb* papers, papering, papered

paragraph *noun* paragraphs

parallel *adjective*

Tip! Double the **l** in **parallel** and keep the last **l** single.

parcel *noun* parcels

pardon *verb* pardons, pardoning, pardoned

pardon *noun* pardons

parent *noun* parents

parishioner *noun*

park *noun* parks

park *verb* parks, parking, parked

parliament *noun* parliaments

parrot *noun* parrots

part *noun* parts

part *verb* parts, parting, parted

partial *adjective*

partiality *noun*

particle *noun* particles

particular *noun* particulars

particularly *adverb*

partly *adverb*

party *noun* parties

pass *verb* passes, passing, passed

You use **passed** in, e.g. *We passed the house*. You use **past** in e.g. *In the past ...*

- ★ A **pail** is a bucket. **Pale** means almost white.
- ✪ A **pain** is an unpleasant feeling caused by injury or disease. A **pane** is a piece of glass in a window.
- ☆ A **pair** is a set of two. A **pear** is a fruit.

pass *noun* passes

passage *noun* passages

passenger *noun* passengers

past *noun, adjective, preposition*

> Watch out! You use **passed** in, e.g. *We passed the house.* You use **past** in, e.g. *It is past six already.*

pat *verb* pats, patting, patted

pat *noun* pats

patch *noun* patches

patch *verb* patches, patching, patched

path *noun* paths

patient *noun* patients

pattern *noun* patterns

pause *noun* pauses

pause *verb* pauses, pausing, paused

paw *noun* paws

paw *verb* paws, pawing, pawed

pay *verb* pays, paying, paid

pea *noun* peas

peace★ *noun*

peaceful *adjective*

peak✪ *noun* peaks

peak *verb* peaks, peaking, peaked

peal *verb* peals, pealing, pealed

peal☆ *noun* peals

pear✤ *noun* pears

pearl *noun* pearls

peasant *noun* peasants

pebble *noun* pebbles

peculiar *adjective*

pedal *noun* pedals

pedal *verb* pedals, pedalling, pedalled

peddle✱ *verb* peddles, peddling, peddled

peer *verb* peers, peering, peered

peer✦ *noun* peers

pen *noun* pens

pencil *noun* pencils

pencil *verb* pencils, pencilling, pencilled

penetration *noun*

penny *noun* pennies or pence

people *noun* peoples

peppery *adjective*

per *preposition*

perceive *verb* perceives, perceiving, perceived

perch *noun* perch

perch *verb* perches, perching, perched

percussionist *noun*

perfect *verb* perfects, perfecting, perfected

perfectly *adverb*

perform *verb* performs, performing, performed

performance *noun* performances

perhaps *adverb*

period *noun* periods

permanence *noun*

permanent *adjective*

permission *noun*

perseverance *noun*

persevere *verb* perseveres, persevering, persevered

persistently *adverb*

person✳ *noun* persons or people

personal *adjective*

persuade *verb* persuades, persuading, persuaded

pet *noun* pets

phone *noun* phones

phone *verb* phones, phoning, phoned

photograph *noun* photographs

photograph *verb* photographs, photographing, photographed

phrase *noun* phrases

phrase *verb* phrases, phrasing, phrased

pick *verb* picks, picking, picked

pick *noun* picks

a b c d e f g h i j k l m n o **p** q r s t u v w x y z

★ **Peace** is a time when there is no war. You use **piece** when you mean a part of something, e.g. *a piece of cake.*

✪ A **peak** (noun) is the top of something. To **peak** (verb) is to reach the highest point. To **peek** is to look secretly at something.

☆ To **peal** is to make a ringing sound of bells. A **peal** is a ringing sound of bells. **Peel** (noun) is the skin of fruit and vegetables. To **peel** (verb) something is to take the skin off it.

✤ A **pair** is a set of two. A **pear** is a fruit.

✱ To **peddle** is to sell things on the street. A **pedal** is something you move with your foot to make something go.

✦ To **peer** is to look closely at something. A **pier** is a long building on stilts going into the sea.

✳ The normal plural for **person** is **people**: *three people came.* **Persons** is formal, e.g. in official reports.

A B C D E F G H I J K L M N O P Q R S T U V W X Y Z

picnic *noun* picnics

picnic *verb* picnics, picnicking, picnicked

picture *noun* pictures

picture *verb* pictures, picturing, pictured

pie *noun* pies

piece* *noun* pieces

> Tip! To remember the spelling, remember you can have a **pie**ce of **pie**!

piece *verb* pieces, piecing, pieced

pierce *verb* pierces, piercing, pierced

piercing *adjective*

pig *noun* pigs

pigeon-hole *noun* pigeon-holes

pile *noun* piles

pile *verb* piles, piling, piled

pillow *noun* pillows

pilot *noun* pilots

pilot *verb* pilots, piloting, piloted

pin *noun* pins

pin *verb* pins, pinning, pinned

pine *noun* pines

pine *verb* pines, pining, pined

pink *adjective* pinker, pinkest

pink *noun* pinks

pipe *noun* pipes

pipe *verb* pipes, piping, piped

pirate *noun* pirates

pistol *noun* pistols

pit *noun* pits

pit *verb* pits, pitting, pitted

pitch *verb* pitches, pitching, pitched

pity *verb* pities, pitying, pitied

place *noun* places

place *verb* places, placing, placed

plague *noun* plagues

plague *verb* plagues, plaguing, plagued

plain *adjective* plainer, plainest

plain *noun* plains

plainly *adverb*

plainness *noun*

plan *noun* plans

plan *verb* plans, planning, planned

plane★ *noun* planes

plane *verb* planes, planing, planed

planet *noun* planets

plank *noun* planks

planner *noun*

plant *noun* plants

plant *verb* plants, planting, planted

plastic *noun* plastics

plate *noun* plates

plate *verb* plates, plating, plated

platform *noun* platforms

play *verb* plays, playing, played

play *noun* plays

player *noun* players

playful *adjective*

playground *noun* playgrounds

plead *verb* pleads, pleading, pleaded

pleasant *adjective* pleasanter, pleasantest

please *verb* pleases, pleasing, pleased

pleasure *noun* pleasures

plenty *noun*

plot *noun* plots

plot *verb* plots, plotting, plotted

plough *noun* ploughs

plough *verb* ploughs, ploughing, ploughed

plumed *adjective*

plunge *verb* plunges, plunging, plunged

plunge *noun* plunges

pocket *noun* pockets

pocket *verb* pockets, pocketing, pocketed

poem *noun* poems

point *noun* points

point *verb* points, pointing, pointed

pointlessly *adverb*

poison *noun* poisons

poison *verb* poisons, poisoning, poisoned

poisonous *adjective*

poke *verb* pokes, poking, poked

pole *noun* poles

police *noun*

✱ You use **piece** when you mean a part of something, e.g. *a piece of cake*. **Peace** is a time when there is no war.

★ A **plane** is an aeroplane, a level surface, a tool or a tree. To **plane** is to make wood smooth with a tool. **Plain** means not pretty or decorated. A **plain** is a flat piece of land.

police officer *noun* police officers

polish *verb* polishes, polishing, polished

polish *noun* polishes

polite *adjective* politer, politest

politely *adverb*

politician *noun* politicians

pomp *noun*

pompous *adjective*

pompously *adverb*

pond *noun* ponds

pony *noun* ponies

pool *noun* pools

pool *verb* pools, pooling, pooled

poor *adjective* poorer, poorest

pop *verb* pops, popping, popped

popular *adjective*

popularly *adverb*

population *noun* populations

porch *noun* porches

port *noun*

poser *noun* posers

position *noun* positions

position *verb* positions, positioning, positioned

possess *verb* possesses, possessing, possessed

possession *noun* possessions

possessor *noun*

possible *adjective*

possibly *adverb*

post *noun* posts

post *verb* posts, posting, posted

pot *noun* pots

pot *verb* pots, potting, potted

potato *noun* potatoes

> Watch out! Add **-es** for the plural, **potatoes**.

potion *noun* potions

pounce *verb* pounces, pouncing, pounced

pound *noun* pounds

pound *verb* pounds, pounding, pounded

pour *verb* pours, pouring, poured

powder *noun* powders

powder *verb* powders, powdering, powdered

power *noun* powers

powerful *adjective*

practice *noun* practices

practise *verb* practises, practising, practised

> **Practice** is a noun and **practise** is a verb, e.g. *music practice, I need to practise more.*

praise *verb* praises, praising, praised

praise *noun* praises

prawn *noun* prawns

pray★ *verb* prays, praying, prayed

prayer *noun* prayers

pre-eminent *adjective*

precede *verb* precedes, preceding, preceded

precious *adjective*

prefer *verb* prefers, preferring, preferred

preference *noun* preferences

prejudiced *adjective*

preparation *noun* preparations

prepare *verb* prepares, preparing, prepared

presence *noun*

present *noun* presents

present *verb* presents, presenting, presented

presently *adverb*

preservation *noun*

preserve *verb* preserves, preserving, preserved

press *verb* presses, pressing, pressed

press *noun* presses

pressure *noun* pressures

pretend *verb* pretends, pretending, pretended

prettiness *noun*

pretty *adjective* prettier, prettiest

prevent *verb* prevents, preventing, prevented

previous *adjective*

prey *verb* preys, preying, preyed

price *noun* prices

price *verb* prices, pricing, priced

pricey *adjective*

pride *noun* prides

prince *noun* princes

princess *noun* princesses

a b c d e f g h i j k l m n o **p** q r s t u v w x y z

★ To **pray** is to say prayers. To **prey** (verb) on animals is to hunt and kill them. **Prey** (noun) are animals that are food to other animals.

A
B
C
D
E
F
G
H
I
J
K
L
M
N
O
P
Q
R
S
T
U
V
W
X
Y
Z

principal★ *noun* principals

principally *adverb*

principle★ *noun* principles

print *verb* prints, printing, printed

print *noun* prints

prise✪ *verb* prises, prising, prised

prison *noun* prisons

prisoner *noun* prisoners

private *noun* privates

privilege *noun*

privileged *adjective*

prize✪ *noun* prizes

prize *verb* prizes, prizing, prized

probable *adjective*

probably *adverb*

Tip! Start with **probable**, and take off the **e** and add **y** to spell **probably**.

problem *noun* problems

proceed *verb* proceeds, proceeding, proceeded

process *noun* processes

process *verb* processes, processing, processed

procession *noun* processions

produce *verb* produces, producing, produced

product *noun* products

professionally *adverb*

professor *noun* professors

Tip! Start with **profess** and add **or**, profess + or = **professor**.

profit☆ *noun* profits

profit *verb* profits, profiting, profited

program✣ *noun* programs

programme✣ *noun* programmes

progress *verb* progresses, progressing, progressed

project *noun* projects

project *verb* projects, projecting, projected

promise *noun* promises

promise *verb* promises, promising, promised

pronounce *verb* pronounces, pronouncing, pronounced

pronunciation *noun* pronunciations

proper *adjective*

properly *adverb*

property *noun* properties

prophesy *verb* prophesies, prophesying, prophesied

prophet *noun* prophets

protect *verb* protects, protecting, protected

protection *noun*

protest *noun* protests

protest *verb* protests, protesting, protested

proud *adjective* prouder, proudest

proudly *adverb*

prove *verb* proves, proving, proved

provide *verb* provides, providing, provided

provincial *adjective*

public *adjective, noun*

publish *verb* publishes, publishing, published

pudding *noun* puddings

puff *verb* puffs, puffing, puffed

puff *noun* puffs

pull *verb* pulls, pulling, pulled

pull *noun* pulls

pulse *noun* pulses

pump *noun* pumps

pump *verb* pumps, pumping, pumped

pumpkin *noun* pumpkins

punch *verb* punches, punching, punched

punch *noun* punches

punctual *adjective*

punctuate *verb* punctuates, punctuating, punctuated

punish *verb* punishes, punishing, punished

punishment *noun* punishments

pupil *noun* pupils

puppy *noun* puppies

purchaser *noun*

★ A **principal** is a head of a college or school and a **principle** is a general rule or truth.
✪ To **prise** something is to open it. To **prize** something is to value it highly.
☆ **Profit** is the extra money got by selling something for more than it costs. A **prophet** is either someone who says what will happen in the future or a religious teacher.
✣ You use **program** when you are talking about computers. In other meanings you use **programme**.

Rr: Try also words beginning with **rh-** or **wr-**

pure *adjective* purer, purest

purple *noun, adjective*

purpose *noun* purposes

purse *noun* purses

pus *noun*

push *verb* pushes, pushing, pushed

push *noun* pushes

put★ *verb* puts, putting, put

> Watch out! The past tense of **put** is **put**.

putt★ *verb* putts, putting, putted

putt *noun* putts

puzzle *noun* puzzles

puzzle *verb* puzzles, puzzling, puzzled

pyramid *noun* pyramids

Qq

qualify *verb* qualifies, qualifying, qualified

quality *noun* qualities

quantity *noun* quantities

quarrel *noun* quarrels

quarrel *verb* quarrels, quarrelling, quarrelled

quarter *noun* quarters

quay✪ *noun* quays

queen *noun* queens

quench *verb* quenches, quenching, quenched

query *noun* queries

query *verb* queries, querying, queried

quest *noun* quests

question *noun* questions

question *verb* questions, questioning, questioned

questioner *noun*

quick *adjective* quicker, quickest

quickly *adverb*

> Tip! Start with **quick** and add **ly**, **quick** + **ly** = **quickly**.

quiet *adjective* quieter, quietest

quietly *adverb*

quite *adverb*

quiver *verb* quivers, quivering, quivered

quiver *noun* quivers

Rr

rabbit *noun* rabbits

race *noun* races

race *verb* races, racing, raced

radio *noun* radios

radioactivity *noun*

raft *noun* rafts

rag *noun* rags

rage *noun* rages

rage *verb* rages, raging, raged

ragged *adjective*

rail *noun* rails

railway *noun* railways

rain☆ *verb* rains, raining, rained

rainbow *noun* rainbows

raise *verb* raises, raising, raised

rambler *noun*

range *noun* ranges

range *verb* ranges, ranging, ranged

rank *noun* ranks

rank *verb* ranks, ranking, ranked

rapid *adjective*

rapidly *adverb*

rapids *plural noun*

rare *adjective* rarer, rarest

rat *noun* rats

rate *noun* rates

rate *verb* rates, rating, rated

rather *adverb*

rattle *verb* rattles, rattling, rattled

rattle *noun* rattles

ravenous *adjective*

ravenously *adverb*

raw *adjective* rawer, rawest

reach *verb* reaches, reaching, reached

reach *noun* reaches

reaction *noun* reactions

read✤ *verb* reads, reading, read

> Watch out! The past tense of **read** is the same spelling but rhymes with **bed**.

★ To **put** something somewhere is to place it there. To **putt** a ball is to tap it gently.
✪ A **quay** is a place where ships tie up. A **key** is a device for opening a lock.
☆ **Rain** is when water drops from clouds. To **reign** is to rule as a king or queen. A **rein** is a strap used to guide a horse.
✤ To **read** is to look at something written or printed.

a b c d e f g h i j k l m n o p q r s t u v w x y z

reading *noun* readings

ready *adjective* readier, readiest

real *adjective*

realistically *adverb*

realize *verb* realizes, realizing, realized

> Tip! You can spell this with **-ize** or **-ise**.

really *adverb*

> Double up! There is double **l** in **really**.

reappear *verb* reappears, reappearing, reappeared

reappearance *noun*

rear *noun* rears

rear *verb* rears, rearing, reared

rearrangement *noun*

reason *noun* reasons

reason *verb* reasons, reasoning, reasoned

reasonable *adjective*

recall *verb* recalls, recalling, recalled

recap *verb* recaps, recapping, recapped

receipt *noun* receipts

receive *verb* receives, receiving, received

> Tip! Use the '**i before e except after c**' rule for **receive**.

recent *adjective*

recite *verb* recites, reciting, recited

reckon *verb* reckons, reckoning, reckoned

recognize *verb* recognizes, recognizing, recognized

recommend *verb* recommends, recommending, recommended

recommendation *noun*

record *noun* records

record *verb* records, recording, recorded

recover *verb* recovers, recovering, recovered

red *adjective* redder, reddest

red *noun* reds

redo *verb*

referee *noun* referees

referee *verb* referees, refereeing, refereed

reference *noun* references

referral *noun*

refine *verb* refines, refining, refined

reflect *verb* reflects, reflecting, reflected

reflection *noun* reflections

refresh *verb* refreshes, refreshing, refreshed

refuse *verb* refuses, refusing, refused

regard *verb* regards, regarding, regarded

region *noun* regions

register *noun* registers

register *verb* registers, registering, registered

regret *noun* regrets

regret *verb* regrets, regretting, regretted

regular *adjective*

regularity *noun*

reign *verb* reigns, reigning, reigned

reign★ *noun* reigns

> Watch out! **E is before i** and there is a silent **g** in **reign**.

rein★ *noun* reins

reiterate *verb*

relate *verb* relates, relating, related

relative *noun* relatives

relax *verb* relaxes, relaxing, relaxed

relaxation *noun*

release *verb* releases, releasing, released

release *noun* releases

relevance *noun*

relevant *adjective*

reliability *noun*

reliable *adjective*

relief *noun* reliefs

relieved *adjective*

religion *noun* religions

reluctance *noun*

remain *verb* remains, remaining, remained

remains *plural noun*

remark *verb* remarks, remarking, remarked

remark *noun* remarks

★ To **reign** is to rule as a king or queen. A **rein** is a strap used to guide a horse. **Rain** is when water drops from clouds.

remember *verb* remembers, remembering, remembered

Tip! To make the past tense, **remember + ed = remembered.**

remembrance *noun*

remind *verb* reminds, reminding, reminded

remove *verb* removes, removing, removed

repayment *noun*

repeat *verb* repeats, repeating, repeated

repeat *noun* repeats

replace *verb* replaces, replacing, replaced

reply *noun* replies

reply *verb* replies, replying, replied

Tip! To make the past tense, change the **y** to **i** then add **ed, replied.**

report *verb* reports, reporting, reported

report *noun* reports

reproductive *adjective*

request *verb* requests, requesting, requested

request *noun* requests

require *verb* requires, requiring, required

rescue *verb* rescues, rescuing, rescued

rescue *noun* rescues

researcher *noun*

resemble *verb* resembles, resembling, resembled

reserve *verb* reserves, reserving, reserved

reserve *noun* reserves

resign *verb* resigns, resigning, resigned

Watch out! There is a silent **g** in **resign**.

resist *verb* resists, resisting, resisted

resistant *adjective*

resolve *verb* resolves, resolving, resolved

respect *noun* respects

respect *verb* respects, respecting, respected

respond *verb* responds, responding, responded

responsibly *adverb*

rest *verb* rests, resting, rested

restlessness *noun*

restoration *noun*

restore *verb* restores, restoring, restored

result *noun* results

result *verb* results, resulting, resulted

resume *verb* resumes, resuming, resumed

retort *verb* retorts, retorting, retorted

retort *noun* retorts

retreat *verb* retreats, retreating, retreated

return *verb* returns, returning, returned

return *noun* returns

reveal *verb* reveals, revealing, revealed

revenge *noun*

revise *verb* revises, revising, revised

revival *noun* revivals

reward *noun* rewards

reward *verb* rewards, rewarding, rewarded

rewrite *verb* rewrites, rewriting, rewrote, rewritten

Watch out! The past tense of **rewrite** is **rewrote**. I rewrote my work.

rheumatic *adjective*

rhyme *noun* rhymes

rhyme *verb* rhymes, rhyming, rhymed

Watch out! There is a silent **h** in **rhyme** and in **rhythm**.

rhythm *noun* rhythms

ribbon *noun* ribbons

rice *noun*

rich *adjective* richer, richest

rid *verb* rids, ridding, rid

ride *verb* rides, riding, rode, ridden

Watch out! The past tense of **ride** is **rode** and the past participle is **ridden**.

ride *noun* rides

rider *noun* riders

ridiculous *adjective*

ridiculously *adverb*

rifle *noun* rifles

a b c d e f g h i j k l m n o p q r s t u v w x y z

A B C D E F G H I J K L M N O P Q R S T U V W X Y Z

right★ *noun* rights

right *verb* rights, righting, righted

rightfully *adverb*

ring✪ *noun* rings

ring☆ *verb* rings, ringing, rang, rung

rip *verb* rips, ripping, ripped

rip *noun* rips

ripeness *noun*

ripple *noun* ripples

ripple *verb* ripples, rippling, rippled

rise *verb* rises, rising, rose, risen

rise *noun* rises

risk *verb* risks, risking, risked

risk *noun* risks

river *noun* rivers

riveting *adjective*

road✤ *noun* roads

roar *noun* roars

roar *verb* roars, roaring, roared

roast *verb* roasts, roasting, roasted

rob *verb* robs, robbing, robbed

robe *noun* robes

robot *noun* robots

rock *noun* rocks

rock *verb* rocks, rocking, rocked

rocket *noun* rockets

rocky *adjective* rockier, rockiest

rod *noun* rods

roll *verb* rolls, rolling, rolled

roll *noun* rolls

roof *noun* roofs

> Watch out! The plural of **roof** is **roofs**.

room *noun* rooms

root* *noun* roots

root *verb* roots, rooting, rooted

rope *noun* ropes

rot *verb* rots, rotting, rotted

rough *adjective* rougher, roughest

roughness *noun*

round *adjective* rounder, roundest

round *noun* rounds

round *verb* rounds, rounding, rounded

route* *noun* routes

row *noun* rows

row✦ *verb* rows, rowing, rowed

royal *adjective*

rub *verb* rubs, rubbing, rubbed

rub *noun* rubs

rubber *noun* rubbers

rubbish *noun*

rude *adjective* ruder, rudest

rudely *adverb*

rug *noun* rugs

ruin *verb* ruins, ruining, ruined

ruin *noun* ruins

rule *noun* rules

rule *verb* rules, ruling, ruled

rumble *verb* rumbles, rumbling, rumbled

rumble *noun* rumbles

run *verb* runs, running, ran, run

run *noun* runs

runner *noun* runners

runny *adjective* runnier, runniest

rush *verb* rushes, rushing, rushed

rush *noun* rushes

rustle *verb* rustles, rustling, rustled

rustler *noun*

- ★ A **right** (noun) is something you are entitled to. To **right** (verb) something is to make it right. A **rite** is a ceremony or ritual. You use **write** in, e.g. *to write a letter*.
- ✪ A **ring** (noun) is a round piece of jewelry. The past tense is **ringed** when you mean to put a ring round something. To **wring** something is to squeeze it hard.
- ☆ A **ring** (noun) is a noise. The past tense is **rang** and the past participle is **rung** when you mean to make a sound like a bell.
- ✤ A **road** is a hard surface for traffic to use. **Rode** is the past tense of **ride**.
- * A **root** is the part of a plant that grows underground. A **route** is the way you go to get to a place.
- ✦ A **row** is a line of people or things and rhymes with 'go'. A **row** is also a noise or argument and rhymes with 'cow'. To **row** means to use oars to make a boat move and rhymes with 'go'.

Ss: Try also words beginning with ce-, ci-, or sc-

Ss

sac★ *noun* sacs

sack *noun* sacks

sack *verb* sacks, sacking, sacked

sacrifice *noun* sacrifices

sacrifice *verb* sacrifices, sacrificing, sacrificed

sad *adjective* sadder, saddest

saddle *noun* saddles

saddle *verb* saddles, saddling, saddled

sadly *adverb*

safe *adjective* safer, safest

safe *noun* safes

safely *adverb*

safety *noun*

sail *noun* sails

sail○ *verb* sails, sailing, sailed

sake *noun*

sale *noun* sales

salt *verb* salts, salting, salted

same *adjective*

sand *verb* sands, sanding, sanded

sandwich *noun* sandwiches

sari *noun* saris

satellite *noun* satellites

satisfaction *noun*

saucepan *noun* saucepans

savage *verb* savages, savaging, savaged

savagery *noun*

save *verb* saves, saving, saved

say *verb* says, saying, said

> Watch out! The past tense of **say** is **said**.

scale *noun* scales

scale *verb* scales, scaling, scaled

scan *verb* scans, scanning, scanned

scan *noun* scans

scarcely *adverb*

scare *verb* scares, scaring, scared

scare *noun* scares

scarlet *adjective*

scary *adjective* scarier, scariest

scatter *verb* scatters, scattering, scattered

scene *noun* scenes

> A **scene** is a place or part of a play. **Seen** is the past participle of **see**.

scent *noun* scents

scent *verb* scents, scenting, scented

scented *adjective*

scheme *noun* schemes

scheme *verb* schemes, scheming, schemed

school *noun* schools

science *noun*

scientist *noun* scientists

scissors *plural noun*

> Watch out! The first 's' sound is spelt **sc** in **scissors**.

scoop *noun* scoops

scoop *verb* scoops, scooping, scooped

score *noun* scores

score *verb* scores, scoring, scored

scorer *noun*

scramble *verb* scrambles, scrambling, scrambled

scramble *noun* scrambles

scrape *verb* scrapes, scraping, scraped

scrape *noun* scrapes

scraper *noun*

scratch *verb* scratches, scratching, scratched

scratch *noun* scratches

scream *noun* screams

scream *verb* screams, screaming, screamed

> Watch Out! The long vowel 'ee' is spelt **ea** in **scream**.

screech *noun* screeches

screech *verb* screeches, screeching, screeched

screw *noun* screws

screw *verb* screws, screwing, screwed

scrub *verb* scrubs, scrubbing, scrubbed

sea☆ *noun* seas

seal *noun* seals

seal *verb* seals, sealing, sealed

search *verb* searches, searching, searched

a b c d e f g h i j k l m n o p q r **s** t u v w x y z

★ A **sac** is a bag-like part of an animal or plant. A **sack** is a large bag. To **get the sack** is to lose your job.
○ A **sail** is a sheet that catches the wind to make a boat go. You use **sale** in, e.g. *The house is for sale.*
☆ A **sea** is an area of salt water. You use **see** in, e.g. *I can't see anything.*

Ss: Try also words beginning with **ce-**, **ci-**, or **sc-**

search noun searches

seasickness noun

season noun seasons

season verb seasons, seasoning, seasoned

seat noun seats

seat verb seats, seating, seated

second noun seconds

second verb seconds, seconding, seconded

secret noun secrets

section noun sections

secure verb secures, securing, secured

security noun

see verb sees, seeing, saw, seen

Watch out! The past tense of **see** is **saw**. The 'or' sound is spelt **aw** in **saw**.

seed noun seeds

seem verb seems, seeming, seemed

seize verb seizes, seizing, seized

Watch out! **E is before i** in **seize**.

select verb selects, selecting, selected

self noun selves

Watch Out! Change the **f** to **ves** to make the plural **selves**.

sell verb sells, selling, sold

Watch out! The past tense of **sell** is **sold**.

send verb sends, sending, sent

Watch out! The past tense of **send** is **sent**.

sensation noun sensations

sensational adjective

sense noun senses

sense verb senses, sensing, sensed

sensible adjective

sensibly adverb

sensitively adverb

sentence noun sentences

sentence verb sentences, sentencing, sentenced

separate verb separates, separating, separated

Watch out! There is an **a** in the middle of **separate**.

separation noun

serial noun serials

series noun series

serious adjective

seriously adverb

servant noun servants

serve verb serves, serving, served

serve noun serves

service noun services

service verb services, servicing, serviced

serviette noun serviettes

set verb sets, setting, set

set noun sets

settle verb settles, settling, settled

several determiner, pronoun

severe adjective severer, severest

sew★ verb sews, sewing, sewed, sewn or sewed

shade noun shades

shade verb shades, shading, shaded

shadow noun shadows

shadow verb shadows, shadowing, shadowed

shaft noun shafts

shaggy adjective shaggier, shaggiest

shake verb shakes, shaking, shook, shaken

shake noun shakes

shall verb should

shallow adjective shallower, shallowest

shame verb shames, shaming, shamed

shape noun shapes

shape verb shapes, shaping, shaped

share noun shares

share verb shares, sharing, shared

shark noun sharks

sharp adjective sharper, sharpest

sharp noun sharps

sharply adverb

★ To **sew** is to work with a needle and thread. To **sow** is to put seed in the ground.

Ss: Try also words beginning with ce-, ci-, or sc-

sharpness *noun*

shatter *verb* shatters, shattering, shattered

she *pronoun*

she'd

Watch out! **She'd** = **she** + **would** or **had**. Add an **apostrophe** between the **e** and **d**.

she'll

Watch out! **She'll** = **she** + **will**. Add an **apostrophe** between the **e** and **l**.

she's

Watch out! **She's** = **she** + **is** or **has**. Add an apostrophe between the **e** and **s**.

shearer *noun*

shears *plural noun*

shed *noun* sheds

shed *verb* sheds, shedding, shed

sheep *noun* sheep

Watch out! The plural of **sheep** is **sheep**.

sheet *noun* sheets

shelf *noun* shelves

shell *noun* shells

shell *verb* shells, shelling, shelled

shelter *noun* shelters

shelter *verb* shelters, sheltering, sheltered

shepherd *noun* shepherds

Watch out! There is a silent **h** in **shepherd**.

shield *noun* shields

shield *verb* shields, shielding, shielded

shift *noun* shifts

shift *verb* shifts, shifting, shifted

shine *verb* shines, shining, shone or, in 'polish' sense, shined

shiny *adjective* shinier, shiniest

ship *noun* ships

ship *verb* ships, shipping, shipped

shirt *noun* shirts

shiver *verb* shivers, shivering, shivered

shiver *noun* shivers

shivery *adjective*

shock *noun* shocks

shock *verb* shocks, shocking, shocked

shoe *noun* shoes

shoot *verb* shoots, shooting, shot

shoot *noun* shoots

shop *noun* shops

shop *verb* shops, shopping, shopped

shoplifter *noun* shoplifters

shoplifting *noun*

shore *noun* shores

short *adjective* shorter, shortest

shortly *adverb*

shortness *noun*

shot

should *verb*

shoulder *noun* shoulders

shoulder *verb* shoulders, shouldering, shouldered

shout *verb* shouts, shouting, shouted

shout *noun* shouts

shove *verb* shoves, shoving, shoved

shovel *noun* shovels

shovel *verb* shovels, shovelling, shovelled

show *verb* shows, showing, showed, shown

show *noun* shows

shower *noun* showers

shower *verb* showers, showering, showered

shriek *noun* shrieks

shriek *verb* shrieks, shrieking, shrieked

shrill *adjective*

shrink *verb* shrinks, shrinking, shrank, shrunk

shrug *verb* shrugs, shrugging, shrugged

shrug *noun* shrugs

shudder *verb* shudders, shuddering, shuddered

shudder *noun* shudders

shuffle *verb* shuffles, shuffling, shuffled

shuffle *noun* shuffles

shut *verb* shuts, shutting, shut

shy *adjective* shyer, shyest

sick *adjective* sicker, sickest

side *noun* sides

side *verb* sides, siding, sided

a b c d e f g h i j k l m n o p q r **s** t u v w x y z

Ss: Try also words beginning with ce-, ci-, or sc-

sideways *adverb, adjective*

sigh *noun* sighs

sigh *verb* sighs, sighing, sighed

sight★ *noun* sights

sight *verb* sights, sighting, sighted

sign *noun* signs

Watch out! There is a silent **g** in **sign**.

sign *verb* signs, signing, signed

signal *noun* signals

signal *verb* signals, signalling, signalled

significantly *adverb*

silence *noun* silences

silence *verb* silences, silencing, silenced

silent *adjective*

silently *adverb*

silk *noun*

silliness *noun*

silly *adjective* sillier, silliest

silver *noun*

similar *adjective*

similarly *adverb*

simple *adjective* simpler, simplest

simply *adverb*

simultaneous *adjective*

sincere *adjective* sincerer, sincerest

sing *verb* sings, singing, sang, sung

Watch out! The past tense of **sing** is **sang**.

single *noun* singles

single *verb* singles, singling, singled

sink *verb* sinks, sinking, sank or sunk, sunk

sink *noun* sinks

sinner *noun*

sir *noun*

siren *noun* sirens

sister *noun* sisters

sit *verb* sits, sitting, sat

site *noun* sites

site✪ *verb* sites, siting, sited

situate *verb*

size *noun* sizes

size *verb* sizes, sizing, sized

skate *noun* skate

skate *verb* skates, skating, skated

skateboarding *noun*

skeleton *noun* skeletons

sketch *noun* sketches

sketch *verb* sketches, sketching, sketched

skill *noun* skills

skin *noun* skins

skin *verb* skins, skinning, skinned

skinny *adjective* skinnier, skinniest

skip *verb* skips, skipping, skipped

skip *noun* skips

skirt *noun* skirts

skirt *verb* skirts, skirting, skirted

skull *noun* skulls

sky *noun* skies

slam *verb* slams, slamming, slammed

slap *verb* slaps, slapping, slapped

slap *noun* slaps

slave *noun* slaves

slave *verb* slaves, slaving, slaved

sleep *verb* sleeps, sleeping, slept

sleepiness *noun*

sleepy *adjective* sleepier, sleepiest

sleeve *noun* sleeves

slice *noun* slices

slice *verb* slices, slicing, sliced

slide *verb* slides, sliding, slid

slide *noun* slides

slight *adjective* slighter, slightest

slightly *adverb*

slip *verb* slips, slipping, slipped

slip *noun* slips

slope *verb* slopes, sloping, sloped

slope *noun* slopes

sloppily *adverb*

slow *adjective* slower, slowest

slow *verb* slows, slowing, slowed

★ **Sight** is different from **site**, which means the place where something is.
✪ **Site** is different from **sight**, which means your ability to see, or something that you see.

slowly *adverb*

slowness *noun*

slyness *noun*

small *adjective* smaller, smallest

smart *adjective* smarter, smartest

smart *verb* smarts, smarting, smarted

smash *verb* smashes, smashing, smashed

smash *noun* smashes

smell *verb* smells, smelling, smelt or smelled

smell *noun* smells

smile *noun* smiles

smile *verb* smiles, smiling, smiled

smoke *verb* smokes, smoking, smoked

smooth *adjective* smoother, smoothest

smooth *verb* smooths, smoothing, smoothed

smoothness *noun*

smugness *noun*

snail *noun* snails

snake *noun* snakes

snap *verb* snaps, snapping, snapped

snap *noun* snaps

snarl *noun* snarls

snatch *verb* snatches, snatching, snatched

snatch *noun* snatches

sneak *verb* sneaks, sneaking, sneaked

sneak *noun* sneaks

sneer *verb* sneers, sneering, sneered

sneeze *verb* sneezes, sneezing, sneezed

sneeze *noun* sneezes

sniff *verb* sniffs, sniffing, sniffed

sniff *noun* sniffs

snort *verb* snorts, snorting, snorted

snort *noun* snorts

snow *verb* snows, snowing, snowed

so *adverb, conjunction*

soak *verb* soaks, soaking, soaked

soap *noun* soaps

soapy *adjective*

sob *verb* sobs, sobbing, sobbed

sob *noun* sobs

society *noun* societies

sock *noun* socks

sock *verb* socks, socking, socked

sofa *noun* sofas

soft *adjective* softer, softest

softly *adjective*

soil *verb* soils, soiling, soiled

soldier *noun* soldiers

Watch Out! The 'j' sound is spelt **dier** in **soldier**.

solemn *adjective*

Watch Out! There is a silent **m** in **solemn**.

solid *noun* solids

solidity *noun*

solidly *adverb*

solve *verb* solves, solving, solved

some *determiner, pronoun*

somebody *pronoun*

somehow *adverb*

someone *pronoun*

something *pronoun*

Watch Out! **Something** is made from **some** + **thing**, do not forget the **e**.

sometimes *adverb*

somewhat *adverb*

somewhere *adverb*

son* *noun* sons

song *noun* songs

soon *adverb* sooner, soonest

sore *adjective* sorer, sorest

sore *noun* sores

soreness *noun*

sorrow *noun* sorrows

sorry *adjective* sorrier, sorriest

sort *noun* sorts

sort *verb* sorts, sorting, sorted

soul *noun* souls

sound *noun* sounds

sound *verb* sounds, sounding, sounded

sound *adjective* sounder, soundest

soundness *noun*

soup *noun* soups

source *noun* sources

sourness *noun*

south *noun, adjective, adverb*

a b c d e f g h i j k l m n o p q r **s** t u v w x y z

★ A **sun** is a large star. A **son** is a male child.

A
B
C
D
E
F
G
H
I
J
K
L
M
N
O
P
Q
R
S
T
U
V
W
X
Y
Z

southern *adjective*

space *noun* spaces

space *verb* spaces, spacing, spaced

spaghetti *noun*

Watch out! There is a silent **h** in **spaghetti**. Double the **t** too!

spare *verb* spares, sparing, spared

spare *noun* spares

spark *noun* sparks

spark *verb* sparks, sparking, sparked

speak *verb* speaks, speaking, spoke, spoken

spear *noun* spears

spear *verb* spears, spearing, speared

special *adjective*

species *noun* species

speech *noun* speeches

speed *noun* speeds

speed★ *verb* speeds, speeding, sped or speeded

spell *verb* spells, spelling, spelt or spelled

spell *noun* spells

spend *verb* spends, spending, spent

sphere *noun* spheres

Watch out! The 'f' sound is spelt **ph** in **sphere**.

spherical *adjective*

spider *noun* spiders

spill *verb* spills, spilling, spilt or spilled

spill *noun* spills

spin *verb* spins, spinning, spun

spin *noun* spins

spirit *noun* spirits

spiritually *adverb*

spit *verb* spits, spitting, spat

spit *noun* spits

spite *noun*

splash *verb* splashes, splashing, splashed

splash *noun* splashes

splendid *adjective*

split *verb* splits, splitting, split

split *noun* splits

spoil *verb* spoils, spoiling, spoilt or spoiled

spoils *plural noun*

spoon *noun* spoons

spoon *verb* spoons, spooning, spooned

spot *noun* spots

spot *verb* spots, spotting, spotted

spray *verb* sprays, spraying, sprayed

spray *noun* sprays

spread *verb* spreads, spreading, spread

spread *noun* spreads

spring *noun* springs

spring *verb* springs, springing, sprang, sprung

spy *noun* spies

spy *verb* spies, spying, spied

square *noun* squares

square *verb* squares, squaring, squared

squareness *noun*

squash *verb* squashes, squashing, squashed

squash *noun* squashes

squat *verb* squats, squatting, squatted

squat *adjective* squatter, squattest

squeak *verb* squeaks, squeaking, squeaked

squeak *noun* squeaks

squeal *verb* squeals, squealing, squealed

squeal *noun* squeals

squeeze *verb* squeezes, squeezing, squeezed

squeeze *noun* squeezes

squirrel *noun* squirrels

stable *adjective* stabler, stablest

stable *noun* stables

stably *adverb*

stack *noun* stacks

stack *verb* stacks, stacking, stacked

staff *noun* staffs

stage *noun* stages

stage *verb* stages, staging, staged

stagger *verb* staggers, staggering, staggered

stain *noun* stains

stain *verb* stains, staining, stained

★ You use **sped** in this way, e.g. *Cars sped past.* and **speeded** in this way, e.g. *They speeded up the process.*

stair★ *noun* stairs

> Watch out! There is **air** in **stair**.

staircase *noun* staircases

stalk *noun* stalks

stalk *verb* stalks, stalking, stalked

stall *noun* stalls

stall *verb* stalls, stalling, stalled

stammer *verb* stammers, stammering, stammered

stammer *noun* stammers

stamp *noun* stamps

stamp *verb* stamps, stamping, stamped

stand *verb* stands, standing, stood

stand *noun* stands

star *noun* stars

star *verb* stars, starring, starred

stare *verb* stares, staring, stared

stare *noun* stares

start *verb* starts, starting, started

start *noun* starts

startle *verb* startles, startling, startled

starve *verb* starves, starving, starved

state *noun* states

state *verb* states, stating, stated

stateliness *noun*

station *noun* stations

station *verb* stations, stationing, stationed

stationary✿ *adjective*

stationery✿ *noun*

statue *noun* statues

stay *verb* stays, staying, stayed

stay *noun* stays

steadily *adverb*

steady *adjective* steadier, steadiest

steady *verb* steadies, steadying, steadied

steak☆ *noun* steaks

steal✦ *verb* steals, stealing, stole, stolen

> Watch out! The past tense of **steal** is **stole**.

steam *verb* steams, steaming, steamed

steel✦ *verb* steels, steeling, steeled

steep *adjective* steeper, steepest

steer *verb* steers, steering, steered

steer *noun* steers

stem *noun* stems

stem *verb* stems, stemming, stemmed

step *noun* steps

step *verb* steps, stepping, stepped

> Watch Out! Double the **p** when adding **ing** and **ed**, **stepping**, **stepped**.

stern *adjective* sterner, sternest

stern *noun* sterns

sternness *noun*

stick *noun* sticks

stick *verb* sticks, sticking, stuck

sticky *adjective* stickier, stickiest

stiff *adjective* stiffer, stiffest

stiffness *noun*

stile *noun* stiles

still *adjective* stiller, stillest

still *verb* stills, stilling, stilled

stir *verb* stirs, stirring, stirred

stir *noun* stirs

stock *noun* stocks

stock *verb* stocks, stocking, stocked

stole

stomach *noun* stomachs

stomach *verb* stomachs, stomaching, stomached

stone *noun* stones or, for the unit of weight, stone

stone *verb* stones, stoning, stoned

stoop *verb* stoops, stooping, stooped

★ A **stair** is one of a set of steps. To **stare** is to look at something without moving your eyes.

✿ **Stationary** means not moving. **Stationery** is paper and envelopes. Remember there is an **e** in **envelope** which is also in **stationery**.

☆ A **stake** is a pointed stick or post. A **steak** is a thick slice of meat.

✦ To **steal** is to take something that is not yours. **Steel** is a metal and to **steel** yourself is to find courage to do something hard.

a b c d e f g h i j k l m n o p q r **s** t u v w x y z

143

A
B
C
D
E
F
G
H
I
J
K
L
M
N
O
P
Q
R
S
T
U
V
W
X
Y
Z

stop *verb* stops, stopping, stopped

> Watch Out! Double the **p** when adding **ing** and **ed**, **stopping**, **stopped**.

stop *noun* stops

store *verb* stores, storing, stored

store *noun* stores

stork *noun* storks

storm *noun* storms

storm *verb* storms, storming, stormed

story *noun* stories

stout *adjective* stouter, stoutest

stoutness *noun*

straight *adjective* straighter, straightest

strain *verb* strains, straining, strained

strain *noun* strains

strand *noun* strands

strange *adjective* stranger, strangest

strangely *adverb*

stranger *noun* strangers

strap *noun* straps

strap *verb* straps, strapping, strapped

stray *verb* strays, straying, strayed

stray *noun* strays

stream *noun* streams

stream *verb* streams, streaming, streamed

street *noun* streets

strength *noun* strengths

> Watch out! There is a **g** in **strength**.

stretch *verb* stretches, stretching, stretched

stretch *noun* stretches

stretchy *adjective*

strictness *noun*

stride *verb* strides, striding, strode, stridden

stride *noun* strides

strike *verb* strikes, striking, struck

strike *noun* strikes

string *noun* strings

string *verb* strings, stringing, strung

strip *verb* strips, stripping, stripped

strip *noun* strips

stroke *noun* strokes

stroke *verb* strokes, stroking, stroked

strong *adjective* stronger, strongest

struggle *verb* struggles, struggling, struggled

struggle *noun* struggles

stubborn *adjective*

stubbornness *noun*

student *noun* students

study *verb* studies, studying, studied

study *noun* studies

stuff *verb* stuffs, stuffing, stuffed

stumble *verb* stumbles, stumbling, stumbled

stump *noun* stumps

stump *verb* stumps, stumping, stumped

stupid *adjective* stupider, stupidest

sty★ *noun* sties or styes

style *noun* styles

style *verb* styles, styling, styled

stylishly *adverb*

subject *noun* subjects

subject *verb* subjects, subjecting, subjected

submarine *noun* submarines

substance *noun* substances

substantial *adjective*

succeed *verb* succeeds, succeeding, succeeded

success *noun* successes

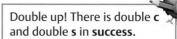

> Double up! There is double **c** and double **s** in **success**.

successful *adjective*

such *adjective*

suck *verb* sucks, sucking, sucked

suck *noun* sucks

sudden *adjective*

suddenly *adverb*

> Watch Out! Double the **d** in **suddenly**.

suffer *verb* suffers, suffering, suffered

sufficient *adjective*

sugar *noun*

 ★ A **sty** is a place for pigs or a swelling on the eye. In the second meaning you can also use *stye*, plural *styes*.

suggest *verb* suggests, suggesting, suggested

suit *noun* suits

suit *verb* suits, suiting, suited

sulkiness *noun*

summer *noun* summers

summon *verb* summons, summoning, summoned

sun★ *verb* suns, sunning, sunned

sunlight *noun*

sunny *adjective* sunnier, sunniest

sunset *noun* sunsets

sunshine *noun*

superior *noun* superiors

supper *noun* suppers

supply *verb* supplies, supplying, supplied

supply *noun* supplies

support *verb* supports, supporting, supported

support *noun* supports

suppose *verb* supposes, supposing, supposed

supposedly *adverb*

sure *adjective* surer, surest

surely *adverb*

surface *noun* surfaces

surface *verb* surfaces, surfacing, surfaced

surge *verb* surges, surging, surged

surge *noun* surges

surprise *noun* surprises

> Watch out! The 'er' sound is spelt **ur** in **surprise**.

surprise *verb* surprises, surprising, surprised

> Watch out! Take off the last **e** when you add **ing** and **ed**.

surround *verb* surrounds, surrounding, surrounded

survive *verb* survives, surviving, survived

suspect *verb* suspects, suspecting, suspected

suspect *noun* suspects

suspicion *noun* suspicions

suspicious *adjective*

swallow *verb* swallows, swallowing, swallowed

swallow *noun* swallows

swamp *verb* swamps, swamping, swamped

swamp *noun* swamps

swarm *noun* swarms

swarm *verb* swarms, swarming, swarmed

swatter *noun*

sway *verb* sways, swaying, swayed

swear *verb* swears, swearing, swore, sworn

sweat *verb* sweats, sweating, sweated

sweep *verb* sweeps, sweeping, swept

sweep *noun* sweeps

sweet *adjective* sweeter, sweetest

sweet *noun* sweets

sweetener *noun*

swell *verb* swells, swelling, swelled, swollen or swelled

swell *noun* swells

swift *adjective* swifter, swiftest

swift *noun* swifts

swiftly *adverb*

swim *verb* swims, swimming, swam, swum

swim *noun* swims

swing *verb* swings, swinging, swung

swing *noun* swings

swirl *verb* swirls, swirling, swirled

swirl *noun* swirls

switch *noun* switches

switch *verb* switches, switching, switched

swoop *verb* swoops, swooping, swooped

swoop *noun* swoops

swop *verb* swops, swopping, swopped

sword *noun* swords

syllable *noun* syllables

sympathy *noun* sympathies

synagogue *noun* synagogues

syrup *noun* syrups

system *noun* systems

a b c d e f g h i j k l m n o p q r **s** t u v w x y z

★ A **sun** is a large star. A **son** is a male child.

A
B
C
D
E
F
G
H
I
J
K
L
M
N
O
P
Q
R
S
T
U
V
W
X
Y
Z

Tt

table *noun* tables

tail *noun* tails

tail★ *verb* tails, tailing, tailed

take *verb* takes, taking, took, taken

tale★ *noun* tales

talent *noun* talents

talk *verb* talks, talking, talked

talk *noun* talks

talker *noun*

tall *adjective* taller, tallest

tangle *verb* tangles, tangling, tangled

tangle *noun* tangles

tank *noun* tanks

tap *noun* taps

tap *verb* taps, tapping, tapped

tape *noun* tapes

tape *verb* tapes, taping, taped

target *noun* targets

target *verb* targets, targeting, targeted

task *noun* tasks

taste *verb* tastes, tasting, tasted

taste *noun* tastes

tea *noun* teas

team⚙ *noun* teams

tear *verb* tears, tearing, tore, torn

> Watch out! The past tense of **tear** is **tore**.

tear *noun* tears

tearfully *adverb*

tease *verb* teases, teasing, teased

telephone *noun* telephones

telephone *verb* telephones, telephoning, telephoned

telescope *noun* telescopes

television *noun* televisions

tell *verb* tells, telling, told

> Watch out! The past tense of **tell** is **told**.

temper *noun* tempers

temple *noun* temples

tempo *noun* tempos

tempt *verb* tempts, tempting, tempted

tend *verb* tends, tending, tended

tender *adjective* tenderer, tenderest

tender *verb* tenders, tendering, tendered

tender *noun* tenders

tensely *adverb*

tension *noun* tensions

tent *noun* tents

term *noun* terms

term *verb* terms, terming, termed

terminate *verb* terminates, terminating, terminated

termination *noun*

terrible *adjective*

terribly *adverb*

terrify *verb* terrifies, terrifying, terrified

territorial *adjective*

terror *noun* terrors

terrorism *noun*

test *noun* tests

test *verb* tests, testing, tested

text *noun* texts

text *verb* texts, texting, texted

than *conjunction*

thank *verb* thanks, thanking, thanked

thanks *plural noun*

that *determiner, conjunction, pronoun*

the *determiner*

theatre *noun* theatres

theatrical *adjective*

theatrically *adverb*

thee *pronoun*

their☆ *determiner*

them *pronoun*

theme *noun* themes

themselves *plural noun*

then *adverb*

there✤ *adverb*

- ★ A **tail** is a part at the back of an animal. A **tale** is a story.
- ⚙ A **team** is a group of people in a competitive game or sport e.g. *a football team*. To be full of, or swarming with, means to **teem**, e.g. *a place teeming with people*. **Teem** also means to pour down.
- ☆ **Their** is different from **there**. *Their pets / I'm going there soon.*
- ✤ **There** is different from **their**. *I'm going there soon / their pets.*

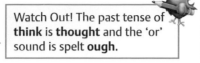

therefore *adverb*

these *determiner, pronoun*

they *pronoun*

> Watch out! The 'ay' sound is spelt **-ey**, **they**.

they'd

> Watch Out! **They'd** = **they** + **had** or **would**. Add an **apostrophe** between the **y** and **d**.

they'll

> Watch Out! **They'll** = **they** + **will**. Add an **apostrophe** between the **y** and **l**.

they're

> Watch Out! **They're** = **they** + **are**. Add an **apostrophe** between the **y** and **r**. Do not confuse with **their** or **there**.

they've

> Watch Out! **They've** = **they** + **have**. Add an **apostrophe** between the **y** and **v**.

thick *adjective* thicker, thickest

thief *noun* thieves

thin *adjective* thinner, thinnest

thin *verb* thins, thinning, thinned

thing *noun* things

think *verb* thinks, thinking, thought

> Watch Out! The past tense of **think** is **thought** and the 'or' sound is spelt **ough**.

thinness *noun*

this *determiner, pronoun*

thistle *noun* thistles

thorough *adjective*

> Watch Out! It is easy to confuse this word with **through**.

thoroughly *adverb*

those *determiner, pronoun*

thou *pronoun*

though *conjunction, adverb*

> Watch Out! The 'oa' sound is spelt **ough** in **though**.

thought *noun* thoughts

thoughtfully *adverb*

thousand *noun* thousands

thread *noun* threads

thread *verb* threads, threading, threaded

threat *noun* threats

threaten *verb* threatens, threatening, threatened

three *noun* threes

thrill *noun* thrills

thrill *verb* thrills, thrilling, thrilled

throne *noun* thrones

through★ *adverb, preposition, adjective*

> Watch Out! The long vowel 'oo' sound is spelt **ough** in **through**.

throughout *preposition, adverb*

throw *verb* throws, throwing, threw, thrown

> Watch out! The past tense of **throw** is **threw**.

throw *noun* throws

thud *noun* thuds

thud *verb* thuds, thudding, thudded

thumb *noun* thumbs

thump *verb* thumps, thumping, thumped

thump *noun* thumps

thunder *verb* thunders, thundering, thundered

thus *adverb*

thy *adjective*

ticket *noun* tickets

tickle *verb* tickles, tickling, tickled

tidily *adverb*

tidiness *noun*

tidy *adjective* tidier, tidiest

tidy *verb* tidies, tidying, tidied

tie *verb* ties, tying, tied

tie *noun* ties

tiger *noun* tigers

tight *adjective* tighter, tightest

a b c d e f g h i j k l m n o p q r s **t** u v w x y z

★ **Through** is different from **threw**, which is a form of the verb **throw**. *Climb through the window. He threw a stone at the window.*

A B C D E F G H I J K L M N O P Q R S T U V W X Y Z

tightly *adverb*

tightness *noun*

tile *noun* tiles

tiled *adjective*

till *noun* tills

till *verb* tills, tilling, tilled

tilt *verb* tilts, tilting, tilted

tilt *noun* tilts

time *noun* times

time *verb* times, timing, timed

timpani *plural noun*

tin *noun* tins

tin *verb* tins, tinning, tinned

tinsel *noun*

tiny *adjective* tinier, tiniest

tip *noun* tips

tip *verb* tips, tipping, tipped

tire★ *verb* tires, tiring, tired

tired *adjective*

title *noun* titles

to✪ *preposition, adverb*

toast *verb* toasts, toasting, toasted

toast *noun* toasts

today *noun, adverb*

toe☆ *noun* toes

toffee *noun* toffees

toga *noun* togas

together *adverb*

tolerable *adjective*

tolerably *adverb*

tolerance *noun*

tolerant *adjective*

tolerantly *adverb*

toleration *noun*

tomato *noun* tomatoes

> Watch out! The plural of **tomato** is **tomatoes**.

tomorrow *noun, adverb*

> Watch Out! There is one **m** and double **r** in **tomorrow**.

tone *noun* tones

tone *verb* tones, toning, toned

tongue *noun* tongues

tonight *adverb, noun*

too✤ *adverb*

tool *noun* tools

tooth *noun* teeth

> Watch out! The plural of **tooth** is **teeth**.

top *noun* tops

top *verb* tops, topping, topped

torch *noun* torches

toss *verb* tosses, tossing, tossed

total *noun* totals

total *verb* totals, totalling, totalled

totally *adverb*

touch *verb* touches, touching, touched

touch *noun* touches

tough *adjective* tougher, toughest

toughly *adverb*

toughness *noun*

tour *noun* tours

toward *preposition*

towel *noun* towels

tower *noun* towers

tower *verb* towers, towering, towered

town *noun* towns

toy *noun* toys

toy *verb* toys, toying, toyed

trace *noun* traces

trace *verb* traces, tracing, traced

track *noun* tracks

track *verb* tracks, tracking, tracked

trade *noun* trades

trade *verb* trades, trading, traded

traffic *verb* traffics, trafficking, trafficked

trail *noun* trails

trail *verb* trails, trailing, trailed

train *noun* trains

train *verb* trains, training, trained

traitor *noun* traitors

tramp *noun* tramps

tramp *verb* tramps, tramping, tramped

transform *verb* transforms, transforming, transformed

translator *noun*

transmission *noun* transmissions

★ To **tire** is to become tired. A **tyre** is a rubber cover for a wheel.
✪ **To** is different from **too** and **two**. *I'm coming to town, too much food, two children.*
☆ A **toe** is part of a foot. To **tow** something is to pull it along.
✤ **Too** is different from **to** and **two**. *I'm coming to town, too much food, two children.*

transport *verb* transports, transporting, transported

trap *noun* traps

trap *verb* traps, trapping, trapped

travel *verb* travels, travelling, travelled

tread *verb* treads, treading, trod, trodden

> Watch out! The past tense of **tread** is **trod**.

tread *noun* treads

treasure *noun* treasures

treasure *verb* treasures, treasuring, treasured

treat *verb* treats, treating, treated

treat *noun* treats

tree *noun* trees

tremble *verb* trembles, trembling, trembled

tremble *noun* trembles

tremendous *adjective*

tribe *noun* tribes

trick *noun* tricks

trick *verb* tricks, tricking, tricked

trickle *verb* trickles, trickling, trickled

trickle *noun* trickles

trip *verb* trips, tripping, tripped

trip *noun* trips

triumph *noun* triumphs

triumph *verb* triumphs, triumphing, triumphed

troop *noun* troops

troop *verb* troops, trooping, trooped

tropical *adjective*

trot *verb* trots, trotting, trotted

trot *noun* trots

trouble *noun* troubles

trouble *verb* troubles, troubling, troubled

trousers *plural noun*

truck *noun* trucks

truly *adverb*

> Watch out! Take the **e** off **true** and add **-ly** to spell **truly**.

trust *verb* trusts, trusting, trusted

truth *noun* truths

try *verb* tries, trying, tried

> Watch out! The past tense of **try** is **tried**.

try *noun* tries

tuba *noun* tubas

tube *noun* tubes

tuck *verb* tucks, tucking, tucked

tuck *noun* tucks

tug *verb* tugs, tugging, tugged

tug *noun* tugs

tumble *verb* tumbles, tumbling, tumbled

tumble *noun* tumbles

tumour *noun* tumours

tune *noun* tunes

tune *verb* tunes, tuning, tuned

tunnel *noun* tunnels

tunnel *verb* tunnels, tunnelling, tunnelled

turn *verb* turns, turning, turned

> Tip! No need to double the **n** when you add **ing** or **ed**, **turning, turned**.

turn *noun* turns

twig *noun* twigs

twig *verb* twigs, twigging, twigged

twin *noun* twins

twin *verb* twins, twinning, twinned

twinkle *verb* twinkles, twinkling, twinkled

twinkle *noun* twinkles

twist *verb* twists, twisting, twisted

twist *noun* twists

twitch *verb* twitches, twitching, twitched

twitch *noun* twitches

two★ *noun* twos

type *noun* types

type *verb* types, typing, typed

typically *adverb*

tyrant *noun* tyrants

tyre✪ *noun* tyres

★ **Two** is different from **to and too**. *I'm coming too, too much food, two children.*
✪ A **tyre** is a rubber cover for a wheel. To **tire** is to become tired.

a b c d e f g h i j k l m n o p q r s **t** u v w x y z

A
B
C
D
E
F
G
H
I
J
K
L
M
N
O
P
Q
R
S
T
U
V
W
X
Y
Z

Uu

ugly *adjective* uglier, ugliest

umbrella *noun* umbrellas

umpire *noun* umpires

unable *adjective*

unavoidably *adverb*

uncomfortable *adjective*

uncontrollable *adjective*

under *preposition, adverb*

underground *noun* undergrounds

underneath *preposition, adverb*

understand *verb* understands, understanding, understood

understandable *adjective*

understandably *adverb*

undo *verb* undoes, undoing, undid, undone

undoubted *adjective*

unfair *adjective*

unfortunately *adverb*

Tip! Start with **unfortunate** and add **ly** to spell **unfortunately**.

unhappy *adjective* unhappier, unhappiest

uniform *noun* uniforms

uninterested *adjective*

unique *adjective*

unit *noun* units

unite *verb* unites, uniting, united

universal *adjective*

unknown *adjective*

unless *conjunction*

unlike *preposition, adjective*

unload *verb* unloads, unloading, unloaded

unlock *verb* unlocks, unlocking, unlocked

unluckily *adverb*

unnaturally *adverb*

unnecessarily *adverb*

unnecessary *adjective*

untidily *adverb*

untidiness *noun*

until *preposition, conjunction*

Watch out! There is only one **l** in **until**.

unusual *adjective*

up *adverb, preposition*

update *verb* updates, updating, updated

upon *preposition*

Watch Out! This word is **up** + **on** = **upon**.

upper *adjective*

upright *noun* uprights

upset *verb* upsets, upsetting, upset

upset *noun* upsets

upstairs *adverb, adjective*

upward *adjective, adverb*

urge *verb* urges, urging, urged

urge *noun* urges

us *pronoun*

use *verb* uses, using, used

use *noun* uses

useful *adjective*

usefully *adverb*

usefulness *noun*

useless *adjective*

usual *adjective*

usually *adverb*

utter *verb* utters, uttering, uttered

Vv

vacant *adjective*

vaccinate *verb* vaccinates, vaccinating, vaccinated

vain★ *adjective* vainer, vainest

valley *noun* valleys

valuable *adjective*

value *noun* values

value *verb* values, valuing, valued

vane★ *noun* vanes

vanish *verb* vanishes, vanishing, vanished

variety *noun* varieties

various *adjective, determiner*

variously *adverb*

vast *adjective*

vegetable *noun* vegetables

vehicle *noun* vehicles

vein★ *noun* veins

velvet *noun*

ventilate *verb* ventilates, ventilating, ventilated

venture *noun* ventures

★ **Vain** means conceited or proud. A **vane** is a pointer that shows which way the wind is blowing. A **vein** carries blood to the heart.

Ww: Try also words beginning with **wh-**

venture *verb* ventures, venturing, ventured

very *adverb, adjective*

> Watch Out! There is only one **r** in **very**.

vessel *noun* vessels

vicious *adjective*

victim *noun* victims

victory *noun* victories

video *noun* videos

video *verb* videoes, videoing, videoed

view *noun* views

view *verb* views, viewing, viewed

vigorous *adjective*

village *noun* villages

villain *noun* villains

violent *adjective*

violently *adverb*

virtue *noun* virtues

visible *adjective*

vision *noun* visions

visit *verb* visits, visiting, visited

visit *noun* visits

visitor *noun* visitors

visual *adjective*

visually *adverb*

vividness *noun*

vocabulary *noun* vocabularies

voice *noun* voices

voice *verb* voices, voicing, voiced

volcano *noun* volcanoes

> Watch out! The plural of **volcano** is **volcanoes**.

volume *noun* volumes

vote *verb* votes, voting, voted

vote *noun* votes

voyage *noun* voyages

Ww

wag *verb* wags, wagging, wagged

wag *noun* wags

wagon *noun* wagons

wagtail *noun* wagtails

wail *verb* wails, wailing, wailed

wail★ *noun* wails

waist✪ *noun* waists

wait *verb* waits, waiting, waited

wait☆ *noun* waits

wake *verb* wakes, waking, woke, woken

wake *noun* wakes

walk *verb* walks, walking, walked

walk *noun* walks

wall *noun* walls

wall *verb* walls, walling, walled

wand *noun* wands

wander *verb* wanders, wandering, wandered

want *verb* wants, wanting, wanted

want *noun* wants

war *noun* wars

wardrobe *noun* wardrobes

wariness *noun*

warm *adjective* warmer, warmest

warm *verb* warms, warming, warmed

warmth *noun*

warn *verb* warns, warning, warned

warning *noun* warnings

warrior *noun* warriors

wary✴ *adjective* warier, wariest

wash *verb* washes, washing, washed

wash *noun* washes

wasn't

> Watch Out! **Wasn't** = was + **not**. Add an apostrophe between the **n** and **t**.

waste *verb* wastes, wasting, wasted

waste✪ *noun* wastes

wasteful *adjective*

wastefully *adverb*

watch *verb* watches, watching, watched

watch *noun* watches

watchfully *adverb*

watchfulness *noun*

★ A **wail** is a loud sad cry. A **whale** is a large sea mammal.
✪ A person's **waist** is the narrow part around their middle. To **waste** something is to use more of it than is needed. **Waste** is also another word for rubbish.
☆ To **wait** is to delay, pause, or rest. A **weight** is how heavy something is.
✴ **Wary** means cautious and careful. **Weary** means very tired.

Ww: Try also words beginning with **wh-**

A B C D E F G H I J K L M N O P Q R S T U V **W** X Y Z

water *noun* waters

water *verb* waters, watering, watered

wave *verb* waves, waving, waved

wave *noun* waves

wax *noun* waxes

wax *verb* waxes, waxing, waxed

way★ *noun* ways

we *pronoun*

we'd

> Watch Out! **We'd** = **we** + **would** or **had**. Add an **apostrophe** between the **e** and **d**.

we'll

> Watch Out! **We'll** = **we** + **will**. Add an **apostrophe** between the **e** and **l**.

we're

> Watch Out! **We're** = **we** + **are**. Add an apostrophe between the **e** and **r**.

we've

> Watch Out! **We've** = **we** + **have**. Add an apostrophe between the **e** and **v**.

weak✪ *adjective* weaker, weakest

wealth *noun*

weapon *noun* weapons

wear☆ *verb* wears, wearing, wore, worn

wearer *noun*

weary *adjective* wearier, weariest

weather *verb* weathers, weathering, weathered

weave *verb* weaves, weaving, weaved or wove, woven

> Watch out! The past tense of is **weaved** or **wove**, e.g. *She weaved her way through the crowd. She wove a shawl.*

web *noun* webs

website *noun* websites

wedding *noun* weddings

weed *noun* weeds

weed *verb* weeds, weeding, weeded

week✪ *noun* weeks

weekday *noun* weekdays

weep *verb* weeps, weeping, wept

weigh★ *verb* weighs, weighing, weighed

weight *noun* weights

> Watch out! The 'ai' sound is spelt **eigh**, and **e before i** is correct in **weight**.

weird *adjective* weirder, weirdest

> Watch out! **E before i** is correct in **weird**.

weirdly *adverb*

weirdness *noun*

welcome *noun* welcomes

welcome *verb* welcomes, welcoming, welcomed

well *noun* wells

well *adverb* better, best

were *verb*

> Watch Out! The past tense of **was** is **were**.

west *noun, adjective, adverb*

wet *adjective* wetter, wettest

wet *verb* wets, wetting, wet or wetted

wetness *noun*

whale *noun* whales

what* *determiner, pronoun*

> Watch out! There is an **h** in **what**.

whatever *pronoun, determiner*

wheel *noun* wheels

wheel *verb* wheels, wheeling, wheeled

when *adverb, conjunction*

★ You can use **way** when asking directions, e.g. *Can you tell me the way?* **Way** can also mean an action, *e.g. Doing it their way*. To **weigh** something is to find out how heavy it is. **Whey** is a watery liquid from milk.

✪ **Weak** means not strong. A **week** is seven days.

☆ To **wear** clothes is to be dressed in them. To **wear** something is to damage it. **Where** is a question word, e.g. *Where are you going?*

* A **watt** is a unit of electricity. You use **what** in a question, e.g. *What are they doing?* or *I don't know what you mean?*

Ww: Try also words beginning with **wh-**

whenever *conjunction*

where★ *adverb, conjunction*

wherever *adverb, conjunction*

whether *conjunction*

which✿ *determiner, pronoun*

> Watch out! There is an **h** in **which**.

while *verb* whiles, whiling, whiled

whine *verb* whines, whining, whined

whine *noun* whines

whip *noun* whips

whip *verb* whips, whipping, whipped

whirl *verb* whirls, whirling, whirled

whirl *noun* whirls

whisk *verb* whisks, whisking, whisked

whisk *noun* whisks

whisper *verb* whispers, whispering, whispered

> Watch out! There is an **h** in **whisper**.

whisper *noun* whispers

whistle *verb* whistles, whistling, whistled

whistle *noun* whistles

white *adjective* whiter, whitest

white *noun* whites

who *pronoun*

who's☆

> Watch Out! **Who's** = who + **is** or **has**. Add an apostrophe between the **o** and **s**.

whoever *pronoun*

whole✤ *noun* wholes

whom *pronoun*

whose *adjective, pronoun*

why *adverb*

wicked *adjective* wickeder, wickedest

wide *adjective* wider, widest

wide *adverb* wider, widest

widen *verb* widens, widening, widened

wife *noun* wives

wild *adjective* wilder, wildest

wild *noun* wilds

wildly *adverb*

will *verb* would

will *noun* wills

willing *adjective*

win *verb* wins, winning, won

win *noun* wins

wind *noun* winds

wind *verb* winds, winding, wound

window *noun* windows

wine *noun* wines

wing *noun* wings

wing *verb* wings, winging, winged

winner *noun* winners

winnings *plural noun*

winter *noun* winters

wipe *verb* wipes, wiping, wiped

wipe *noun* wipes

wire *noun* wires

wire *verb* wires, wiring, wired

wisdom *noun*

wise *adjective* wiser, wisest

wish *verb* wishes, wishing, wished

wish *noun* wishes

wispy *adjective*

wistfulness *noun*

wit *noun* wits

witch *noun* witches

> **Which** is used to ask a question, e.g. *Which one is that?* A **witch** is someone who uses witchcraft.

with *preposition*

> Watch Out! There is no **h** in **with**.

withdraw *verb* withdraws, withdrawing, withdrew, withdrawn

within *preposition, adverb*

without *preposition*

witness *noun* witnesses

wizard *noun* wizards

wolf *noun* wolves

woman *noun* women

a b c d e f g h i j k l m n o p q r s t u v **w** x y z

153

★ To **wear** clothes is to be dressed in them. To **wear** something is to damage it. **Where** is a question word, e.g. *where are you going?*

✿ **Which** is used to ask a question, e.g. *Which one is that?* A **witch** is someone who uses witchcraft.

☆ **Who's** is different from **whose**, e.g. *Who's next in the queue? Whose coat is this?*

✤ You use **whole** in, e.g. *I saw the whole film.* A **hole** is a gap or opening.

Ww: Try also words beginning with **wh-**

A B C D E F G H I J K L M N O P Q R S T U V W X Y Z

won't

> Watch Out! **Won't = will + not**. Add an **apostrophe** between the **n** and **t**.

wonder *verb* wonders, wondering, wondered

wonder *noun* wonders

wonderful *adjective*

wood★ *noun* woods

wooden *adjective*

wool *noun*

woollen *adjective*

woollens *plural noun*

woolly *adjective* woollier, woolliest

word *noun* words

word *verb* words, wording, worded

work *verb* works, working, worked

work *noun* works

worker *noun* workers

world *noun* worlds

worldliness *noun*

worm *noun* worms

worm *verb* worms, worming, wormed

worried *adjective*

worrier *noun*

worry *verb* worries, worrying, worried

worry *noun* worries

worship *verb* worships, worshipping, worshipped

worst *adjective, adverb*

worth *adjective, noun*

would★ *verb*

wouldn't

> Watch Out! **Wouldn't = would + not**. Add an **apostrophe** between the **n** and **t**.

wrap *verb* wraps, wrapping, wrapped

wrap *noun* wraps

wreck *verb* wrecks, wrecking, wrecked

wreck *noun* wrecks

wrecker *noun*

wren *noun* wrens

wrench *verb* wrenches, wrenching, wrenched

wrench *noun* wrenches

wriggle *verb* wriggles, wriggling, wriggled

wriggle *noun* wriggles

wrinkle *noun* wrinkles

wrinkle *verb* wrinkles, wrinkling, wrinkled

wrinkled *adjective*

wrist *noun* wrists

write✿ *verb* writes, writing, wrote, written

> Watch out! The past tense of **write** is **wrote**.

wrong *noun* wrongs

wrong *verb* wrongs, wronging, wronged

wrongly *adverb*

Yy

yard *noun* yards

yawn *verb* yawns, yawning, yawned

yawn *noun* yawns

year *noun* years

yeast *noun*

yell *noun* yells

yell *verb* yells, yelling, yelled

yellow *noun* yellows

yellow *adjective* yellower, yellowest

yes *interjection*

yesterday *noun, adverb*

yet *adverb, conjunction*

yolk *noun* yolks

you *pronoun*

you'd

> Watch Out! **You'd = you + would** or **had**. Add an **apostrophe** between the **u** and **d**.

you'll

> Watch Out! **You'll = you + will**. Add an **apostrophe** between the **u** and **l**.

young *adjective* younger, youngest

★ **Wood** is material from trees or a lot of trees growing together. You use **would** in, e.g. *Would you like to come to tea?*

✿ You use **write** in, e.g. *to write a letter*. A **right** (noun) is something you are entitled to. To **right** (verb) something is to make it right. A **rite** is a ceremony or ritual.

youngster *noun* youngsters

your *determiner*

you're

> Watch out! Do not confuse **you're** and **your**. **You're** = **you** + **are**. Add an apostrophe between **u** and **r**.

yours *pronoun*

yourself *pronoun* yourselves

youth *noun* youths

you've

> Watch out! **You've** = **you** + **have**. Add an **apostrophe** between **u** and **v**.

Zz

zero *noun* zeros

zest *noun*

zone *noun* zones

zoo *noun* zoos

zoology *noun*

a b c d e f g h i j k l m n o p q r s t u v w x y z

Index

157

Index